THE BATTLE OF THE LITTLE BIGHORN

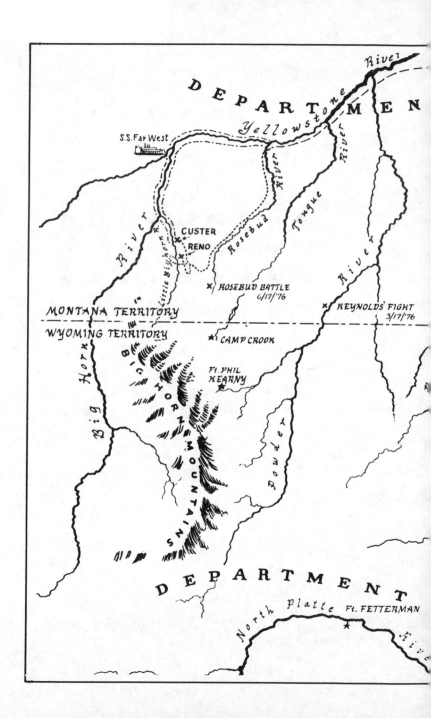

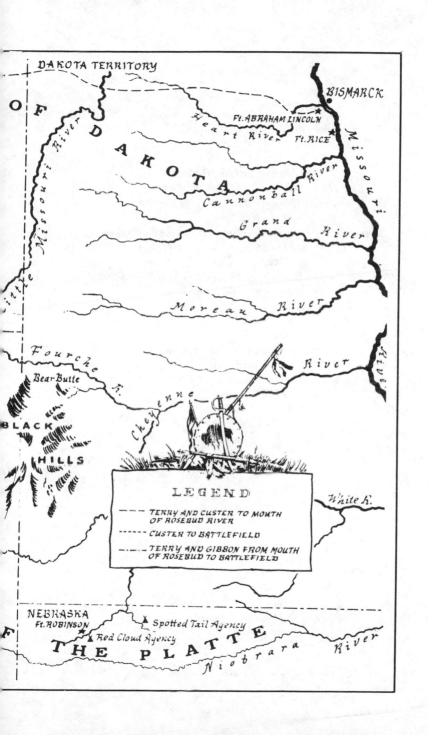

Books by Mari Sandoz published by
the University of Nebraska Press

The Battle of the Little Bighorn
The Beaver Men: Spearheads of Empire
The Buffalo Hunters: The Story of the Hide Men
Capital City
The Cattlemen: From the Rio Grande across the Far Marias
Crazy Horse: The Strange Man of the Oglalas
The Horsecatcher
Hostiles and Friendlies: Selected Short Writings of Mari Sandoz
Love Song to the Plains
Miss Morissa: Doctor of the Gold Trail
Old Jules
Old Jules Country
Sandhill Sundays and Other Recollections
Slogum House
Son of the Gamblin' Man: The Youth of an Artist
The Story Catcher
These Were the Sioux
The Tom-Walker
Winter Thunder

MARI SANDOZ

»▶ »▶ »▶ »▶ »▶ »▶ »▶ »▶ »▶

THE BATTLE OF
THE LITTLE
BIGHORN

★ ★ ★ ★ ★ ★ ★ ★ ★ ★ ★

A BISON BOOK

UNIVERSITY OF NEBRASKA PRESS
LINCOLN AND LONDON

First Bison Book printing: 1978

Most recent printing indicated by first digit below:

7   8   9   10

Library of Congress Cataloging in Publication Data

Sandoz, Mari, 1896–1966.
  The Battle of the Little Bighorn.

  "Bison book edition."
  Reprint of the ed. published by Lippincott, Philadelphia.
  Bibliography: p. 185
  Includes index.
  1. Little Big Horn, Battle of the, 1876.   I.   Title.
[E83.876.S2   178]   973.82   78–8733
ISBN 0–8032–9100–0

Bison Book edition reprinted by arrangement with J. B. Lippincott Company.

Manufactured in the United States of America

"I heard the alarm, but I did not believe it. I thought it was a false alarm. I did not think it possible that any white men would attack us, so strong as we were."

—Account of Custer fight by Low Dog, Oglala Sioux chief.
Leavenworth Weekly Times, August 18, 1881.

CONTENTS

★ ★ ★ ★ ★ ★ ★ ★ ★

MAPS

THE BATTLE OF THE LITTLE BIGHORN

★ ★ ★ ★ ★ ★ ★ ★ ★

»▶ »▶ »▶ »▶ »▶ »▶ »▶ »▶

1 DEPARTURE
FROM THE
YELLOWSTONE

★ ★ ★ ★ ★ ★ ★ ★

There was little to suggest the usual heat and dust of June in the Yellowstone River country this noontime. The sky hung low and gray. The northwest wind, still raw from the hailstorm of the night before, swept over the sagebrush and blew the manes and tails of the horses as the bearded Brigadier General Terry* and his staff, Colonel Gibbon and Major Brisbin, rode out to a ridge and waited. Off below, at the bivouac of the 7th Cavalry, the trumpets sounded "Boots and Saddles," the call thin and fading but golden against the wind.

The command of twelve troops approached, the head of the column rising out of the bottoms, led by Lieutenant Colonel†

---

* Full names and ranks of the military men mentioned in the text are listed at the end of the text, pp. 183–184.

† Current official rank is used in the narrative here, as in all official communications, references, and signatures. Custer (Major General, USA, 1865, by breveted temporary rank) is lieutenant colonel of the 7th Cavalry under Colonel Samuel Davis Sturgis. In

George Armstrong Custer in buckskin and a whitish, flat-topped plains hat, his adjutant, Lieutenant Cooke, beside him, the huge Canadian with long side whiskers swept back by the wind. Behind them rode the standard-bearer, pushing hard against the staff of the swallow-tailed banner—red and blue with the crossed silver-white sabers of Custer's personal emblem—whipping against the sky. Saluting, the commander of the 7th reined up beside the waiting reviewers. The chorus of trumpets broke from the bottoms, the forked guidons streaming over the faded blue of the column that moved smartly up the rise in fours, the shod hoofs already stirring dust from the drying earth. The trumpeters swung their gray horses out beside Custer and halted, their shining song to escort the regiment as it passed.

First came the scouts, headed by the young West Pointer, Lieutenant Varnum. With him rode two well-known plainsmen, Mitch Bouyer and Charley Reynolds. The swarthy Mitch, who was in half-Indian dress, knew every Sioux camp ground, every lodgepole trail from the Musselshell down to the forks of the Platte River. Lonesome Charley Reynolds, who had carried Custer's news of gold located in the Black Hills to the world in 1874, was promised another message of great import on this expedition. So he joined, too, even with an infected hand—his gun hand—in a sling. Behind them jogged a group of other civilians, among them Herendeen, the courier that Terry sent along to bring a scouting report back to him; the two official interpreters, bewhiskered Girard and the Negro Isaiah Dorman, both long in the Missouri River trade; and two realtives of Custer's—he was really sneaking them past—a brother, Boston, listed as quartermaster employee, and the seventeen-year-old nephew, Autie Reed.

The Indian scouts rode in a body, sometimes passing each

narrative reference the qualifying "lieutenant" is usually dropped; in conversation the complimentary highest rank attained by an officer is commonly used.

other or drawing back, the men still chanting from their usual circling ride before any departure to a fight. The ponies varied in color from dun to bay and black, some spotted like the hail drifts that had still gleamed in the breaks when the sun rose, some of the horses painted and feathered for war. Custer's favorite scout, Bloody Knife, wore white-man shirt and pants, his loose hair held down by a twist of flannel about the head, with three feathers rising from the back. The other two dozen Arikaras looked much the same, all dark-faced and moody ever since they reached the mouth of the Rosebud on the Yellowstone, so far from their earthen villages on the Missouri, so deep in the country of their powerful enemy, the western, the Teton Sioux, and in the time of the great annual gathering from all the Plains.

The six Crow Indians were taller and gayer, more carefree, perhaps because they were headed toward their own country, where they knew every canyon and snakehead gully that led to home. There was a correspondent along, too, although specifically forbidden by Sherman, General of the Army. It was Terry's duty to enforce Sherman's order in this as well as in the refusal, practically to the last minute, to let Custer go with his regiment, yet somehow the general permitted the news-paperman, Mark Kellogg, to slip past on his mule.

Behind Varnum's men came the rhythmic thud of shod hoofs, the creak of leather, the jingle of bit and thump of slung carbines as the blue stream passed, two and two, troop by troop, followed by a small herd of extra horses and finally the dainty-footed mules of the pack train, their inexpertly tied loads already slipping, the animals straggling along, one nipping a bit of grass here, another there, some stopping entirely or deciding to run back to their wagon mates left at the river, the noncoms of the train guard sweating with effort and embarrassment, the civilian packers unconcerned and insolent.

Once more the trumpets came up to send their call to the

wind and to glisten as they were lowered. Then the Gray Horse
Troop moved forward into the column headed off on the five-
day scout ordered by Terry. The route laid out was up the Rosebud Valley to verify the direction of the Indian trail that Major
Reno had just located for Custer and to scout Tullock's Creek
and the upper Tongue River, heading off any Indians trying
to escape southward. This was also to give Gibbon's infantry
time for the march from the Yellowstone by way of the Big
Horn River and up the valley of the Little Bighorn, meeting
Terry late on the 26th or on the 27th. From the headwaters of
the Tongue, Custer was to turn northward across the divide
to the Little Bighorn and move down the stream to the junc-
tion with Terry on the 27th, the fifth day of the scout. Between
the two forces the hostile Sioux would be cracked like a nut
in a vise, or, as one of the friendly Sioux scouts said, "Maybe
like the weak little flea between the fingernails," his eyes looking far away as he spoke.

When the regiment was gone—all except a couple of the
pack mules running down a washout—the colonel clasped the
hands held out to him there on the ridge and wheeled his horse
to overtake his command. Gibbon called out after him, "Now,
Custer, don't be greedy. Wait for us!"

Custer lifted his gauntleted hand in acknowledgement. "No!"
he shouted back, "I–I won't!" his stammer very slight, the am-
biguity left hanging like a puff of pipe smoke over the shoulder
as he galloped off, the wind whipping the color of his standard
behind him.

The clouds thinned and drifted apart in the dying wind. The
sun burned down on the column moving in sections along the
broad valley, fragrant here and there with wild roses still a pink
cascade in late-blooming patches. Blackbirds sang in the rushes
and now and then an awkward shitepoke rose from a marshy
bend, or perhaps a deer started up a slope, looking back. The

scouts burned to take up the chase, to make money as they had on the trail from Fort Abraham Lincoln on the Missouri to the Yellowstone encampment: two dollars apiece for the hind-quarters, a dollar for a forequarter or a saddle—fresh meat for the command. The scouts had earned hundreds of dollars on the way, but now there was to be no shooting at all, not even the pistol's casual bark, except at the enemy. None carried the silent bow, and besides, game would be scarce up where the large Indian camps had been. Perhaps one of the Arikaras, the Rees, would make a bow to get venison for Colonel Custer, who liked it roasted over the coals, as Young Hawk understood so well.

The march of this June 22, 1876, was a weary one, even up the pleasant Rosebud Valley. Last night had been like the usual eve of a military expedition's departure on the Plains, many of the men, particularly the officers, getting little or no sleep. Besides, half of the troops and many of the horses and mules were worn from the long scout under Reno, returning downstream only day before yesterday, and already back on the trail again.

When the bluffs began to push in closer upon the small, clear-watered creek, the command slowed and finally halted on an open bottom along the left, the night-wind side of the creek, where the prevailing west wind blew the mosquitoes to the far bank. They made camp in a patch of timber at the foot of a steep shielding bluff only eleven or twelve miles out, but this, as Reno had reported, was one of the last lush stretches of grass before they reached the deserted campsites of the Sioux, where the valley, the bluffs, and the upland were cropped bare by the vast pony herds of the Indians, the lodgepole trail leading up the creek wide and deeply worn.

There was deadwood for the squad fires here, and the fine smell that even army coffee can send far out to toll the hungry.

Thin streaks of smoke clung along the bluffs an hour before
the lagging pack train was finally whipped in—strung out over a
mile, goods and most of the expedition's ammunition handy for
any Sioux charging out of the willows with waving blanket and
stinging arrow. But somehow none seemed around anywhere
today.

After the early supper the men scattered over the ground,
many napping or already asleep when the shadows crept out
of the cuts and canyons to push the sunlight back. A trumpet
blew officers call; men rose here and there, some from their
troop bivouac, some stretching wearily as they moved through
the shadows to the low fire at Custer's tent, the only tent
except pup halves in the command. The men settled around
the colonel's bed, everybody there from Major Reno down to
the greenest second lieutenant—including some who had
charged the enemy at Custer's side before and perhaps even
had their winter tents burned when their haste did not equal
the commander's urgency.

To the older campaigners, Custer seemed less elated this
evening than usual by tracks of an enemy ahead, certainly less
overflowing with assurance and self-sufficiency than on his strike
against the Cheyennes at the Washita eight years ago. There
seemed unease about him standing there, even flanked as he
was by his brother Captain Tom Custer and his brother-in-law,
Lieutenant Calhoun, with Boston Custer and the nephew off to
the side, and his favorites around him. Cooke, in the adjutant's
position, was at his elbow, Keogh nearby and the Michiganders
too—Weir (like Custer, earlier from Ohio, and a strength to
him when rebellion against Custer broke out in the 3rd Michigan Cavalry in 1865); Yates, also from the Michigan Volunteers; and, farther over, the young and imaginative Harrington,
his strained face often kept in shadow.

One civilian always up close was Mark Kellogg, to catch every word and report it to Bennett of the New York *Herald*, long a backer of the bold commander of the 7th Cavalry who had proved an even bolder commander of the pen, not only for the *Herald*, but, some said, as the author of the May 4 New York *World* attack on Grant for his treatment of Custer. According to the *World's* account, the Secretary of War and General Sherman had gone to the President to protest his treatment of the colonel, Sherman saying that Custer was the only man fit to lead the expedition against the Indians. At Grant's angry demand for an explanation, Sherman wrote a long disclaimer of the whole story. Such a protest had never been made, nor had he ever expressed or intimated the sentiments attributed to him. He believed the army possessed hundreds who were competent to lead the attack on the Indians. As General of the Army he was well aware that Terry had already been appointed to head the expedition.

Now at his tent on the Rosebud, and even though topped by his big adjutant, Custer looked very tall in the firelight creeping up the fringed buckskin to his intense, wind-burned face with its reddish bristles. The sockets of his eyes deepened in the shadows as he gave out directions about troop distribution and formation if the camp were attacked, directions so elementary they clearly hid some more significant purpose, particularly in a regiment that had campaigned nine years with practically the same officers, without one such rudimentary council or instruction. The review seemed more proper to a green regiment out on a more dangerous mission than scouting. Perhaps it was for the benefit of Kellogg, the young law student serving as war correspondent, but the older officers looked uneasy.

Then suddenly the tone of the commander changed, his stammer more evident. He was always willing to accept recommendations from even the junior second lieutenant of the regiment, but such recommendations must come in proper form. He was perfectly aware that his official actions had been discussed and criticized to the Department staff by some here. Now such criticism must cease or proceedings would be initiated against the offenders as provided in the army regulations.

There was a moment of embarrassed silence among the men not of Custer's family or favor, particularly with civilians present —a stunned silence among the newer officers. The tenth-year men, those with the regiment from its first summer, realized that the charge probably lay upon them, no telling where. Finally Captain Benteen of the cropped gray curls spoke up. As everyone knew, his relation to the colonel had not always been the warmest, but as everyone also knew, he was a soldier who did a soldier's duty.

"General,"* he said, "will you not be kind enough to inform us of the names of the offending officers?"

The commander had his reply ready, speaking deliberately, his stammer almost entirely hidden. "While I am not here to be catechized by you, Colonel Benteen," he said, "I take pleasure in informing you, for your own gratification, that you are not among the officers alluded to."

Yet somehow this did not seem enough under the bright evening sky of the shadowed Rosebud, and Custer pushed himself on to the unusual, the unprecedented extreme of explaining himself, asking cooperation from the troop commanders in measures obviously their minimal duty, such as husbanding the rations and conserving the strength of their horses and mules. The command might be out much longer than the five days planned, he said. He intended to follow the trail until they got the Sioux, even if it took them "to the Indian agencies on the Missouri River or in Nebraska," including the latter—although all the men realized that General George Crook, commander

* Complimentary use of former highest rank in conversation, as Custer calls Benteen colonel.

of the Department of the Platte, had been out south of the Yellowstone country since winter and was surely somewhere around the headwaters of the Tongue or the Rosebud right now with his fifteen troops of cavalry and five companies of infantry. Neither Custer nor his officers knew that five days earlier, Crazy Horse, with only part of the hostile Indians, had driven Crook back from the upper Rosebud—Crook, who had whipped the Apaches and sent part of his force to destroy Two Moon's Cheyenne and Sioux camp on the Powder River last March. What most men listening at Custer's fire must have realized was that only Terry's intercession with the infuriated President Grant had restored the colonel to his regiment at all, and at least one knew that Custer in his immediate elation had told Captain Ludlow of the Engineers (with him to the Black Hills in 1874) that he would cut loose from Terry now as he, Custer, had got away from Stanley in the railroad survey of the Yellowstone in 1873.

To his frank determination upon a personal Indian chase even as far as Nebraska, Custer added that there would be no more trumpet calls. "Boots and Saddles" would be at five, each troop commander responsible for his men in all but the start and the camp selections. Then the colonel offered his staff one more surprise: he asked for suggestions that might expedite the march. Once more the men before him moved in uneasiness, puzzled, particularly those who understood the accumulated desperation of the last few months and realized that the coming glories of this centennial summer, this 100th celebration of the Declaration of Independence, promised no shining place in the nation's finest show for George Armstrong Custer. The image of the adored young hero of 1862 and 1868 was now, in 1876, so tarnished that Custer could be ordered to go smell out Indians for the success of Terry and even Gibbon. There were some here on the Rosebud who realized that Custer must feel trapped in the confining dimensions of the scout laid out for him, as trapped as a great winged eagle forced into a cage, making wild and desperate thrusts against the confining bars, breaking plumage, talons, and beak.

Few of Custer's staff would risk making suggestions, even to his public request. Afterward they walked back to their troops, alone or in twos and threes—silent mostly, a few in low, sparse talk. Lieutenant Wallace, regimental recorder and only four years out of West Point, fell in beside Captain Godfrey, an old-timer with the 7th.

"I believe General Custer is going to be killed," the young man finally said, his voice barely rising above the swish of boots through the grass. "I never heard him talk that way before."

At the Indian camp, on a little rise to catch any night breeze that might carry a remote sound to their ears, and away from the sour smell of the sweaty white men, some of the scouts were gathered around a handful of coals for a thoughtful smoke. Custer's Bloody Knife, the Ree-Sioux, and Half Yellow Face, the Crow, were bridging the language gap with sign talk, considering what might happen, what seemed certain to happen. As Godfrey came by, they inquired if he had ever fought the Sioux. To his show of confidence in the regiment, one of the Crows reminded him this was the foe who had wiped out the arrogant Fetterman about ten years ago and less than one day's hard riding to the southward.

Even Mitch Bouyer was not convinced that the 7th could whip the Sioux. "One goddamn big fight," he predicted, with a Frenchman's shrug of the shoulder, and went out to look along the bluffs for the day scouts, yet to come in to the late supper.

The disquiet among the officers lasted long after they left Custer's tent. Several little knots of them were still talking low and seriously when the thin horns of the new moon settled into the hazy west. Many of them had not slept at all the previous night. The *Far West*, the shallow draft stern-wheeler steamboat carrying the headquarters of Terry's expedition, was anchored in the Yellowstone near the mouth of the Rosebud. Tom Custer and Calhoun had played poker on board until dawn with Keogh, the Irish soldier of fortune. They left IOU's behind, although the paymaster, at Custer's orders, had accompanied the command to the first camp out of Fort Abraham Lincoln.

"To avoid the whisky sellers getting the two months' pay," was Custer's explanation at the time, but his feud with the post trader was well known. Besides, there were whisky sellers all along the route and several around last night to grab what was left of any loose pay, from the new recruit's thirteen dollars a month on up. Much of the money had been sent back to Fort Lincoln and beyond by the mail couriers from the camps on the way west, or spent with the trader wagons along the Yellowstone, for hunting ammunition or big hats against the sun, but mainly for whisky. The army poker players usually kept their money handy, particularly in the 7th, with enough recklessness in the regiment to bring complaints against Custer for permitting, even encouraging, the gambling that was the ruin of many young officers.

But not everyone on the *Far West* spent last night at poker. Some of the officers made their wills, the adventurous Keogh among them. Others left verbal instructions for the disposition of property and mementoes if they did not return.

Custer had been in conference with Gibbon and Terry on the boat when the hailstorm struck the regiment, whitening the prairie like winter snow and leaving the air chilled into the next day. The men in the cabin of the *Far West* had understood the military, political, and financial nature of the problem very well: the hostile Sioux under Sitting Bull and Crazy Horse refused to leave their ancient and treaty-sanctioned hunting ways for life on the reservations. Now these Indians must be driven from all the Yellowstone country, swept out to clear the way for the Northern Pacific Railroad, which had been stopped at the Missouri by lack of funds in the panic years of the early 1870's. Custer's 1874 expedition had been intended to locate the gold known to be in the Black Hills, and to bring in a rush of railroad investors and gold seekers. The gold was found but the investors did not come. Still, removal of the Indians would bring them and release the railroad snorting impatiently at the Missouri. With the Sioux gone from the Yellowstone Valley, the way would be open to the gold mines of Alder Gulch and Virginia City, Montana—open for new gold strikes, too, and new range for the Longhorn herds bellowing their way north from Texas. Chiefly, however, the urgency was for the gold and its magic with the centers of powerful finance, American and European.

General Terry had seen the reports sent around the Departments of Dakota and the Platte in April and early May, verifying that there were three thousand lodges of hostile Indians in the Yellowstone country. He knew this meant 3,500 to 4,000 warriors at the least, more against an attack, with every male from twelve to eighty a fighter in defense of the villages. Terry understood the starvation on the reservations that drove the Indians out to the buffalo ranges as soon as the ponies strengthened with new grass, even if no courier reached him with the late May report that the Sioux agencies down in Nebraska were almost deserted, that eight hundred to a thousand agency warriors had secretly gone north to join Crazy Horse. Every old-timer in the region, red and white, knew that more Indians would go for the summer sun dance and great annual Teton Council, including all the western Sioux. Anticipating such powerful numbers had justified General Crook's move out of the south to the upper Tongue River country with a force of well over a thousand men when winter still held the Indians. Custer's activities in the East had delayed the command from the north; but now, four months late, Terry and Gibbon with their strong forces were to reach the Little Bighorn late the 26th, while Custer scouted the Rosebud and the Tongue.

After the conference on the *Far West*, Terry and Gibbon had accompanied Custer to the bivouac, the night white as with snow, the hail crunching under their boots. At his tent they shook hands and left, wishing him good luck. Custer was irritable and apparently full of apprehension, although both men had been as helpful as possible. Gibbon, despite his own command's needs, gave up his best guides, including the Sioux breed, Bouyer, and six of his Crow scouts, men of the Yellowstone country who had hunted and fought Sioux all over the region.

General Terry had been generous all spring. He had requested that Grant let Custer return to his regiment for the expedition against the Sioux, despite the President's anger over Custer's volunteered testimony in the army tradership investigations, which were planned, many thought, to give the Democrats their first chance to elect a President since the Civil War. Even the investigators labeled the Custer testimony hearsay, with no firsthand information. Although the Secretary of War had already resigned, Custer did emphasize Belknap's gag rule against army officers and cited the "banishment of Colonel Hazen to Fort Buford, 1,000 miles up the Missouri," as punishment for his protests against farming out post traderships and the profiteering on the common soldier.

There was some surprise at this praise of Hazen, for Custer had shown animosity against him ever since, as Officer of the Day, Hazen had placed young Custer under arrest at West Point for one of his many infringements of the rules. Besides,

Hazen was sent into the Black Hills in 1867—seven years before Custer, who since 1874 had publicly prided himself as being the first into the Hills. In addition, Hazen was General Terry's choice to lead the expedition against the Sioux if Custer had not been permitted to return to his post. Intentional or not, Custer's charge that Hazen had been banished for protesting graft in traderships summoned him before the investigators, too, and held him in Washington when he should have taken command at Fort Abraham Lincoln.

More infuriating, however, to the President than Custer's charges of graft and rake-offs against the already disgraced and departed Belknap were the accusations, also hearsay, against half a dozen prominent army men and Grant's own brother, in addition to other charges against Lewis Merrill, major of the regiment, and even Sturgis, colonel of the 7th Cavalry. The President was certainly aware that Custer was involved in the New York *Herald* articles denouncing Belknap and the whole Administration, some perhaps actually written by the ambitious Custer during this presidential election year, when it seemed that practically any Democrat might be elected. Besides, Grant must have known that Custer himself stood accused, by hearsay, of graft and attempts at graft through post traders all the way from Texas to Fort Lincoln and beyond. It was a time of graft, insubordination, and disobedience.

But with May upon them, and General Crook in the field for months, the expedition from the north must move, the 7th Cavalry, commanded by Major Reno while Sturgis was on detail duty in Washington, with it. Custer was urged to go directly to the President. But Grant refused to see him, either while arrogant or after some awkward attempts at a halfhearted penitence. So Terry suggested that Custer wire the President, begging to be spared the humiliation of seeing his regiment march without him. To this Terry appended a note and re-

ceived a reply from General of the Army Sherman saying that
he could take Lieutenant Colonel Custer on the expedition if
he wished, but adding: "Advise Custer to be prudent, not to
take along any newspapermen, who always make mischief, and
to abstain from personalities in the future . . ." It was a few
hours after Custer received this news that he told Captain
Ludlow he intended to "cut loose" from Terry. Ludlow immediately spoke of this to fellow officers, perhaps uneasy about
the campaign and angry at Custer's arrogance toward a superior
who had gone to such lengths to restore him to the regiment.

After the disastrous months just passed, Custer knew it was
time to place himself above his enemies. With the convenient
memory of the ambitious, he apparently recalled the extrav-
agant praise of the winter and made something of the usual
toast to "a future president." And why not? Such ambition was
the privilege of every native male, intensified by the serious
political interest common to every high officer of the army in
these uncertain years. Custer's interest in national politics was
an old one. In 1860, while at West Point, he wrote at length
about the presidency.* Then in 1866 he had ridden Johnson's
train in the President's hopeless campaign to win support for
his Reconstruction plans and a favorable Congress. Custer had
spoken from the rear platform and heard the applause of the
crowd. Often enthusiasm was much greater for the young major
general than for Johnson, and sometimes shrill shouts demanded

* Letter, May 5, 1860, to a friend at New Rumley, Ohio, dis-
cussing the coming presidential election: "It . . . will result in the
utter defeat of the Republicans and I hope in the complete demo-
lition of the Republican Party. Although I am far from being a
Douglasite I believe he would make a good president, there are
others I would prefer to him, I would like to see either Dickinson
of this state, Lane of Oregon or Hunter of Virginia receive the
nomination. I am satisfied however that the party will yet unite on
a good man and that man is destined to be the next president . . ."
signed GA Custer. (Reprinted with permission of Michael Ginsberg.)

Grant and Custer instead of the President. And then came last winter's entertainments by the newspapers and railroads, and the flattering, if perhaps hollow, suggestion for the national ticket this election year—not Grant but Custer.

So last night, June 21, Custer had returned to his tent from the *Far West* and prepared to march in the morning. Still nervous and irritable, he abolished his own recent division of the regiment into two six-troop wings commanded by Reno and Benteen. From now on, every troop commander would report directly to him. This reduced Benteen to his one troop and left Reno, less than a month ago commander of Fort Abraham Lincoln and the 7th Cavalry, with no unit at all, only his personal striker and a cook, both from Keogh's I Troop.

A pool of around 155 or 160 mules had been selected from the wagon train (left behind at the Yellowstone) with each troop assigned twelve animals to pack the rations, enough for fifteen days instead of Terry's planned five. Each trooper would carry 100 rounds of ammunition for his carbine and 24 for the pistol in addition to 12 pounds of oats for his horse. The extra regimental ammunition—24,000 rounds—was packed on the twelve strongest mules.

Some of the commanders questioned these loads for the fast pace Custer outlined. The mules from Reno's long, swift march up beyond the forks of the Powder, over to the Tongue and down the Rosebud, and just in yesterday, were worn. Overloaded, they would break down.

Custer had cut the complaints short. "Gentlemen, you may carry what supplies you please. You will be held responsible for your companies," he said, and elaborated on the arduous route and pace he planned. Then, as he entered his tent, he turned his head back to advise the men they had better carry an extra supply of salt. "We may have to live on horsemeat before we get through. Probably mule meat, unless some men are left to walk or many saddles are emptied."

After the conference the officers scattered, mostly to the Far West, some to a night of cards and whisky, some to stories and song. Once Reno and the lieutenant of the boat's guard stood together, arms around each others shoulders, singing "Larboard Watch."

Custer also returned to the boat. Major James S. Brisbin, commanding Gibbon's cavalry and considered an officious old blatherskite by some, complained to Terry about "the insufferable ass, the wild man" that the general was turning loose up the Rosebud in pursuit of the Sioux, and urged that the four troops of his 2nd Cavalry be added to the 7th, Terry to go as commander of the combined column.

The general refused. Custer smarted under a rebuke from the President, he said, and wanted an independent campaign and a chance to do something.

When Brisbin still persisted, Terry stopped his protests. "You don't seem to have confidence in Custer."

"None in the world," Brisbin replied. "I have no use for him." Yet he received permission to approach Custer with the idea. Custer refused, saying he had everything he needed in his regiment. As a homogeneous body it would accomplish as much as the two commands combined. Plainly, he welcomed no superior along, not even General Terry.

To Brisbin's offer of Low's battery of rapid-fire Gatling guns Custer agreed, but an hour later he returned to say, bluntly, "I won't want Low. I am afraid he will impede my march with his guns."

Aware that the general was sending Custer farther around to delay his arrival at the Little Bighorn to meet Gibbon's infantry coming up the river, Brisbin urged Custer to reconsider. Without replying, the colonel went to Terry with his refusal of the Gatlings. They were drawn by condemned cavalry horses, much to slow to keep pace with his troops, he said.

Apparently the general was unwilling to push the need for

delay or was convinced that the guns wouldn't slow the march. Probably he was still humoring his ambitious subordinate for private and unexplainable reasons.

Now, after the short march of June 22 to the first bivouac on the Rosebud, it was clear that even condemned cavalry horses would have kept up with the ragged, disintegrating pack train and that the Gatlings would have been useful in holding off a fast warrior charge that could sweep away the poorly protected mules strung out miles behind the command. But Custer's decision stood, no matter how gnawed over by the officers, like coyotes worrying an old buffalo skin.

Finally the last uneasy officer settled down to the stir of insects and the weary snores in the patch of timber. Few privates, except the sentries, lay awake tonight, not even for the coyotes, very noisy, with the high, thin yip of young ones among them, or for the farther, deeper howl of the prairie wolves, nor even to listen for Sioux war whoops that would surely be heard soon—perhaps at dawn tomorrow, or before. Several men who wandered off to the latrine area went beyond, slipping horses out past the weary guard. Perhaps they were afraid of Indians, but more probably they were drawn to the gold boom over southeast, in the Black Hills. Like earlier deserters, back near Custer's old trail into the Hills, they knew that Deadwood Gulch was full of motley miners where a man could lose himself as easily as he could kick his cavalry mount in the belly, send the horse running into the timber, or perhaps even trade it to brand blotters, as he could trade his pistol for a pair of civilian pants.

Custer had scouts out in twos and threes, searching the night, but the Ree, Bloody Knife, had gone alone, unofficially, missing soon after supper. No one admitted he knew where the Knife had gone, although several realized he had obtained a flask of whisky, either from Mark Kellogg, who stopped him earlier to ask questions, or from one of the officers wishing to cheer the expert scout out of his growing gloom. Plainly the liquor must be taken away from the camp, and so Bloody Knife disappeared to his horse and into the hills, perhaps to think about the long-time enmity between his parental peoples, the Rees and the Sioux, and about the annual Teton council, of the seven divisions of western Sioux that had met at Bear Butte near the Black Hills until last year, until driven off by the miners of Deadwood. He knew that this year the call gathered them somewhere south of the Yellowstone, both the hostile and the agency Sioux with thousands of warriors. Surely he thought about Custer and about the colonel's talk to the Rees at Fort Lincoln and later at Young Man Butte, the seventh camp on the expedition. Both times Custer told them this was to be his last campaign and so he must win a victory. A victory now, even if only against five or six lodges of the Sioux, would make him the President, the Great Father in Washington, and he must turn back as soon as he had won. He would take Bloody Knife to Washington with him and then send him home again to a fine house built for him. All the Ree scouts would have plenty to eat for all time to come.

". . . you and your children," he had told them.

But now it was plain that this white-man war chief was leading them not against a few lodges but upon the great annual summer gathering of all the Teton Sioux, the people whose power the Rees had felt so often. With Custer were the scouts that Bloody Knife had encouraged to come along. Perhaps because the load of this knowledge—the danger he had put upon his brother Rees—was too heavy, Bloody Knife had slipped away, welcoming the forgetting in the whisky, not to return until after dawn, stumbling, leading his horse, still too drunk for the saddle.

As ordered, there was no reveille for the regiment the 23rd. At three o'clock the horseguards fumbled around in the dark shaking the troops from their sleep. The scouts—Ree, Crow, and white—were already gone with Varnum. At five the column moved out, Custer leading, followed by the two color sergeants. The reorganized pack train was massed near the end of the command, with Benteen and three troops bringing up the rear to collect the straggling and straying mules, pick up the scattered packs.

By now the bluffs pushed in close upon the Rosebud. Within the first three miles the command made five crossings of the thin string of water, often with deep mud and marsh in the bends. Finally the valley opened out once more. Five miles on, brush and timber spotted the pleasant bottoms, crowded in around the feet of the bluffs, and trailed up the deeper ravines. Custer found some of his scouts waiting here, at the Rosebud trail and one of the campsites that Reno had seen on his scout. There were many packed-earth circles where lodges had stood and many remains of wickiups—bent ribs of willow sticks and brush still tied together at the top and once covered with robes or blankets—the low temporary shelters for extra youths and warriors. Some of the troops, the recruits raw to the country, even a few of the officers, thought these were shelters for dogs, perhaps misled by all the tracks of wolves and particularly coyotes, the scavengers of any deserted camp. Many of the men did not understand the difference between the Missouri River tribes and other reservation Indians, with their rabble of dogs, and the Indians out on the prairies, where one bark could betray a small camp to an overwhelming enemy. The troopers might have noticed the reaction of the scouts with the column. Dark and stony-faced, their moccasins soft on the worn earth of the camp, they moved from the large central circle where the council lodge had stood to the skeleton of the farthest wickiup in the brush. They examined the thick scattering of bones, particularly the larger ones, cracked for the marrow. They kicked these aside to send the bugs scurrying, talking quietly about the number and kinds; they considered the earth under the fire spots for the length of burning.

The scouts out ahead reported that the grass was eaten off short for miles around, the earth dotted with the droppings of thousands of horses, droppings beetle-worked and dry. At the upper end of the camp the tracks converged into a broad trail, cut deep by unshod hoofs and raked by thousands of dragging lodgepoles, all headed upstream.

Custer gathered the scouts to him and listened to what he might detect beyond the interpreters, beyond the sign talk, his bearding, sun-flushed face skeptical. Afterward he sent the scouts ahead in two parties and then talked to Varnum alone.

"Here's where Reno made the mistake of his life," the colonel said. "He had six troops of cavalry and rations enough for a number of days. He'd have made a name for himself if he'd pushed on after them."

Yes, if he had pushed on after the Sioux, but it would have been against orders, for he was on a scout, his finding to be reported.

Some distance beyond the first Indian camp the column passed more such sites, one in practically every creek bend, all about the same age, as though the Sioux had moved many times in one day and somehow burned the wood and grazed the hills as well as ate the tons of meat once on the scattered bones. Surely the Rees, the Crows, and the Missouri Sioux, like White Cloud, as well as Mitch Bouyer and Charley Reynolds, knew that these were different villages, different bands, gathering to a great conference. Some of the more observant noticed that as the campsites increased, the Indians with the command began to turn the heads of their horses toward each other, faces set, only the eyes moving, sliding quickly from one to another in secret knowledge, apparently not reassured by the evidence that these camps all seemed to be at least three weeks old and that the Indians might be scattered long before now. Plainly there was uneasiness among the scouts—not only in the taciturn Bloody Knife but in all the traditional enemies of the Sioux who were with him.

Custer hurried on, his dust-reddened eyes focused on the far bluffs up the Rosebud, his ears closed to the warning of his scouts. He forded the creek when necessary and pushed ahead like a hungry wolf on a hot trail. After making thirty-three miles, the command crossed to the right bank and camped at about four-thirty, early enough for the grazing that the horses needed badly. Across the stream the hills rolled back, lightly timbered, with deep ravines that might cover an ambushing enemy, even an attacking Indian army.

Out of the general uneasiness a man was sent back down the Rosebud to hunt for Benteen, somewhere far behind with the pack train. It had taken an hour and a half to get the inexpert outfit through the first crossing. By then Custer's column had been out of sight, at least six miles ahead of the reserve ammunition. With over 150 mules scattered out for almost a mile, Benteen, an experienced Indian campaigner, realized that a handful of warriors whooping out of the nearest canyon could stampede the mules as easily as they could a flock of sheep. They would get at least part of the train, probably the ammunition, packed on the mules that were plainly the best.

With his eyes on the rim of the creek bluffs much of the time, Captain Benteen decided he must have better control of the mule train than from the rear, as ordered by Custer. He sent one troop to flank the head section of the pack string, one to protect the center, and remained with the third, riding guard around the rear. Through increased orderliness he made better progress, but in concentrating on the mules, he came near losing Dr. Lord, one of the regimental surgeons. The doctor grew so seriously ill that he fell behind the packs, far out of sight, and barely managed to drag himself into camp after dark. His ailment was not the only such case in the command. There were few without some sign of trail colic, for which whisky was the accepted palliative, if not the specific. The infection was widespread. On the *Far West* up on the Yellowstone, Gibbon lay stricken with the infection, unable to join his plodding infantry until the 26th.

Benteen managed to cover the day's march four hours behind the column. While Cooke, the regimental adjutant, with his long chop whiskers bristling at the tardiness, designated the camp space for the train and its guard, Benteen told him of the troubles with the mules and the packers, and the changes he had made in the disposition of his troops to protect the train. He asked the adjutant, a favorite of Custer's, to report the liberties he had taken with the orders of the morning.

"I will not tell General Custer anything about it," Lieutenant Cooke replied with his usual brusqueness. "If you want him to know, you must tell him of it yourself."

Fires were ordered extinguished immediately after supper, most of the men asleep before the late twilight was gone and the stars clear. At daybreak the 24th, the Crow scouts reported to Custer that they had found fresh sign of Indians, only three or four horseback and one man afoot, but the trail ahead was broader and fresher too. Excited by the news, the commander did not hold himself to the pace of even the main column but struck ahead with two companies* that were still fairly well mounted. As he rode past the bivouac of the mule guard, Ben-

* The terms "troop" and "company" were used interchangeably to designate the same tactical unit until 1880.

teen reported what he had done about the pack train and its
supplies yesterday.

The commander seemed to take it calmly, in his larger pre-
occupation. "I am much obliged to you, Colonel Benteen," he
said. "I will direct the officer who relieves you today to guard
the train in the same manner."

Then, with his colors fluttering in the rising breeze toward
sunup, Custer headed on up the stream, riding very fast, the
recruits among his men understanding as never before why
their commander was called Hard Backsides, understanding with
admiration. Many stationed along the dull Missouri River posts
for several years were eager for the first Sioux war whoop.

The stable sergeants had their constant worries over forage
for the stock of the command, well over eight hundred head,
not counting the horses of the various civilians, and this with
the grass eaten into the ground. The Indians and other scouts
were worried too: their horses had to cover substantially more
miles than those of the regiment. Six Indians were sent out to
hunt up remote low spots and bottoms for grass for their
hungry ponies, grass preferably rich in seed to be gathered into
their blankets and bundled tight with the lariats.

There was a continued scarcity of game too; even the blackbirds were gone from their nesting marshes, with little sign of
life anywhere except for the magpies scavenging the old campsites and a buzzard or two circling. The greenness of the broken
branches around the camps, the growing freshness of the pony
droppings, and the wind-blown ashes of the fires told the scouts
and even some of the troopers how swiftly Custer was overtak-
ing the Indians. Finally the column reached a large, grazed-
over stretch, the grass eaten bare for many miles out over the
low hills and along the pretty valley of the Rosebud. Plainly,
the camp here had been occupied for some days. Out on the

bottom stood the bare frame of a large circular sun dance arbor, the pine boughs browning and brittle, the center pole still up with some tatters flying at the top where the buffalo image and other ceremonial objects had hung. On a stick thrust into the ground was the dried scalp of a white man, perhaps of the one 2nd Cavalry trooper killed sometime ago during Gibbon's march down the Yellowstone to the meeting place. It was taken to Custer and then passed around the angry men of the command, and ended up in Sergeant Jeremiah Finley's saddlebags. He was one of the older line sergeants of the regiment and perhaps was given first right.

There were other things more disturbing than one scalp to the scouts, both Rees and Crows, and certainly to the Sioux, who understood much of what had happened here from what was left behind. On a sand bar they found pictures drawn with a stick, perhaps a message for Indians to come past that way. The Sioux scouts slumped in their saddles a long while, speaking low, making signs.

"The pictures say an army is coming . . ."

In one of the dismantled sweat lodges, much like the remains of the low wickiups but with stones that had been fire-heated and then doused with water, sand had been heaped in a long ridge and pictures drawn along it, shod-hoof prints—meaning Custer's cavalry, the scouts thought—on one side, the pony tracks of the Sioux on the other. Between them lay many dead men, their heads toward the tracks of the Indians.

The Rees, of a small sedentary tribe long raided by the powerful Sioux, were very disturbed, certain that the enemy medicine was too strong for the soldiers and that they would all be defeated. This was fortified, they said, by stones left in another sweat lodge—three stones painted red and set in a row, meaning in Sioux sign language that the Great Powers had promised them victory and if the whites did not come for them, the Indians would search them out. In thanksgiving for these assurances, four upright sticks held a buffalo calfskin that had been adorned with cloth and other articles of value as gifts to the Great Powers, White Cloud, the Sioux scout, explained.

Probably none of the officers gathered in a curious half-circle on their horses at the sun dance place knew it was Sitting Bull who had danced here for guidance, for the wisdom to stop the white man pushing in with guns destroying the buffalo and miners digging up the sacred earth of Paha Sapa, the Black Hills. Now the white man's fire wagon that tore through the silence across the Platte country of the south was roaring its impatience at the Missouri, the path already laid out to the gold fields of the western mountains up along the Yellowstone, the final arrow to pierce the heart of the Indian country.

Certainly the scouts—at least the Sioux—knew from the symbolic pictures that the dreamer was Sitting Bull; that here, after giving one hundred bits of skin from his arms and staring into the sun for two days while he danced, he had received the vision pictured on the sand ridge of the sweat lodge: soldiers falling head first into his camp—many, many soldiers. This news had surely been signaled to the last of the young men on the agencies, from those in west Nebraska to those of the upper Missouri—a special inducement to obey the call to the great annual Teton council even though it was away from the sacred Bear Butte. More would slip away, as their fellows had been doing all spring, eager for the promise in the Hunkpapa medicine man's vision, certain now that the move of the council from the Sacred Bear near the Black Hills to the Little Bighorn was sanctioned as good.

So the trail up the Rosebud had grown even wider, deeper, as a river grows when fed by many springs.

Nor did Custer or his Indian scouts know that barely a week

ago a war party of these Indians had faced General Crook's army only a few miles up the Rosebud and that, for the first time in history, the Sioux had attacked in something like an organized battle charge, led by a war chief whose name, Crazy Horse, was scarcely known up around Fort Abraham Lincoln. Some may have heard of him almost ten years ago, when he led the decoy party that brought the end of the willful and disobedient young Lieutenant Fetterman.

There were darkening looks and low, angry words among the Rees, too, as they realized where the great enlarging trails led. For perhaps 150 years the Sioux had met at Bear Butte, just above the Black Hills. Since Custer's report of "gold at the grass roots," two years earlier, miners ran like ants over the rocks and burrowed into the earth of the Hills, many so near that, with the wind right, the loud whoop of a gold strike around Deadwood Gulch could be heard at the Butte of the Crouching Bear. Until last year, for two summer weeks the rolling hills around there lay dark as in brooding cloud-shadows with the twenty–thirty thousand ponies of the Sioux, while thousands of lodges stood in the forks of Bear Butte Creek in the seven circles of the Tetons. Many tame Indians, those from the trader forts and the agencies, came too, taking their traditional places for this ancient ceremonial, this ancient counciling that the Tetons brought west. It was a time of excitement, with racing, wrestling, dancing, singing, drumming, and always the formal ceremonials in the great center lodge made with poles eighteen feet tall from the deep canyons of the Black Hills. Here in this vast lodge, the chiefs of all the Tetons met to plan the year for the entire nation.

Now, since they were driven from Bear Butte, they were gathering somewhere up ahead in all their power, with many allies as guests, many Northern Cheyennes, some Arapahos, and perhaps a band of eastern Sioux, too, old Inkpaduta and his small following of Waist and Skirt people.*

Custer ordered coffee boiled and summoned his officers to where the guidon was stuck into the earth, whipping in the hot southerly wind. Once more it was an awkward conference, possibly because the commander was irritable and unsure, perhaps because he felt disapproval in the air. Many of the officers were jumpy, perhaps certain they were involved in open disobedience to Terry's orders. They knew about the early-morning Crow report of what looked like smoke over the ridge at Tullock's Fork, the creek that General Terry had ordered Custer to scout, with Herendeen along to carry the news of the findings back to the general from there.

The men listened to Custer's description of the trail ahead, freshening hourly, he said, but the scouts still found no scattering anywhere, none of the bands leaving for a hunt or perhaps a raid against the Crows or the Shoshonis. Instead, the trail that increased like a burgeoning river was now fed by a deep new one of many riders, their tracks thick and plain over the older lodgepole furrows that headed toward the ancient route across the divide to the Little Bighorn, the Greasy Grass of the Sioux. The trail was six inches deep in fine dust and half a mile wide in places, with the tracks of vast pony herds, and surely more of these farther out, for grass.

Dismissing the sign over Tullock's Creek as morning mist and ignoring Terry's orders to scout the region, Custer commanded the regiment to take the trail ahead but to proceed with increased caution, each troop to march a slightly different route to cut down the dust that would be so detectable from far off.

As the officers started toward their men, the wind blew

* A division of the Sioux.

Custer's standard down, toward the rear. Captain Godfrey recovered it, only to see it fall toward the rear once more. A second time he rescued the banner from the dust, this time digging the staff into the baked earth, supporting it against a sturdy sagebrush. The flag stood now, its swallowtails sagging; but Godfrey, from Custer's native Ohio and a stalwart admirer, was disturbed by the double fall rearward, as were others who saw it—an omen of defeat at this crucial time.

Custer led his force out, ignoring the warning and the growing sullenness of his scouts—both Crow and Ree, including Bloody Knife, his long-time friend and trusted wolf, as a superior scout was called. He paid no attention to the quiet caution of Charley Reynolds or the louder complaint of Mitch Bouyer. Spurring on, he kept the column strung out behind him, moving as fast as the weary horses could manage, the lagging pack train once more miles behind, the packers and the trooper guard stopping, with sweat and curses, to gather up the scattered packs, to whip the mules on, now that the Indians seemed closer every hour. Probably few of the raw recruits thought of anything beyond the ache of their burning saddle galls, the soreness of their swollen, blistered faces. The doctors did what they could to keep the men comfortable in spite of dust and alkali and buffalo gnats, swarming and tiny as circling dust particles, biting the eyelids until they swelled half-shut, the ears until they were thick as florid saucers. Old-timers knew that the Indians smeared themselves thick with bear grease and ashes against the pests and that freighters and hunters spread bandannas under their hats with a spot of coal oil on each flapping corner.

Even without deer flies to drive the horses crazy, and the gnats, the march would have been hot and dusty, with repeated halts necessary to let the scouts keep ahead. To Custer's exasperation, his Indians traveled more and more slowly as the trail freshened. Some looked back from one rise after another, anxious to keep within range of immediate support, even support whose adequacy they plainly doubted. The sun burned down through the sweated gray-blue shoulders of the troopers, although the buckskin of Custer and some of the other officers was even more airless, the soft surface thick with dust in spite of the staggered order of march.

Around four o'clock several of the Crows returned. They had been out on some of the stronger army horses and reported another trail, only a day or two old, of a large band of Indians from the south. These had not followed the regular route from the Nebraska agencies—down the Tongue—but crossed the Rosebud above the sun dance site and struck the trail where it turned toward the Little Bighorn, which was not over thirty miles ahead, moving with precision as though by guide or very accurate direction.

Custer, with his orderly carrying the guidon, took the information to the Ree camp. The Indians were sitting in a half-circle, the pipe of council going around. Custer joined them, resting on one knee, and asked about the report of the Crows, speaking, as always, with less impediment to the Indians.

"They tell me there are large camps of the Sioux," he said. "What do you suppose will be the outcome?"

Stabbed, the adviser, the medicine man among them, jumped up and hopped around in a bullet-dodging dance to show how the Indian saved himself while the troops stood still to be shot down like buffalo calves. Other officers came to listen at the smokeless little council fire, hearing Custer tell the Rees that all he expected of them in the fight was to capture as many Sioux horses as they could get, all for themselves. He ended by repeating his promise to befriend the Rees in Washington if the campaign was successful, the promise that he had elaborated to Bloody Knife and the others of the tribe long ago.

About five in the afternoon Custer led the regiment forward once more, across the Rosebud, the stream's left bank ridged by uncountable lodgepoles. The trail grew steadily deeper, with fresher, later travel. About seven forty-five in the evening, after twenty-six miles for the day, the command halted below a steep bluff, hidden as well as possible from all but the early croak of the frogs and the far howl of the coyotes, starting very early, the Rees remarked, as before a big hunt, a big meat-making. The troopers were ordered to keep their fires small as the scouts' little nest of coals, and soon dead. The mules were left under packs, the horses saddled, some trying to roll in the dust to rid themselves of the day's sweat and weariness, the recruits of the horse guard struggling with them under the curses of their sergeants, trying to keep them from scattering so swiftly to the first real grass they had found—grass now because here the Indian trail went on and on, without a stop.

A whisper ran through the bivouac like a little night wind talking to itself: the scouts were hurrying out on the trail beyond the turn toward the Little Bighorn, where the command was to meet Gibbon and Terry, maybe the day after tomorrow. Old campaigners predicted that, if the trail really crossed the divide, the regiment would march tonight. Major Reno, still without a troop to command, was silent, almost an outsider, less than a bystander with the regiment he had led so recently.

After the frugal and hasty meal, Captain Keogh and his lieutenant, James E. Porter, had come over to Benteen's bivouac, where four–five officers were sitting around listening to Lieutenant De Rudio's yarns in his heavy Italian-English, yarns of campaigns in other wars in other lands. Benteen brushed the dust from his curly graying hair, set his saddle up for a pillow, spread the saddle blanket, and notified the rest that he was going to pick up a little sleep, for surely they would not be camped here all night.

Around ten o'clock an orderly from regimental headquarters came to call the officers to Custer's tent. By now the sliver of early moon was gone; the night was darkened by the pattern of fireflies off toward the creek, the sound of arrow hawks falling upon their prey loud in the silence between the creak of saddle leather and the nose-clearing snorts of the stomping horses.

Benteen directed his first sergeant to see that everything was ready for an immediate march, and joined the other officers stumbling through the tangle of brush, with snoring troopers stretched out anywhere. At Custer's tent they were told that the Crow scouts had come in to confirm the expected direction of the fresh trail that they estimated at about four hundred lodges, with, counting those in wickiups, perhaps 1,500 warriors. Custer passed the figure on with no reference to the Indians of the earlier trail or to the Ree warning of the great annual Teton gathering up ahead. The march was to be resumed at eleven, to get as near as possible before daylight, with time to select the best possible concealment for the day.

Lieutenant Hare and his K Troop were put on duty with the scouts. The other officers aroused their bivouacs, calling the sergeants, low at first, then raising their voices, and finally receiving shouted replies from the darkness off along the bluffs. Horses stomped and whinnied; mules brayed: the peculiar carrying qualities of the hee-haws would attract wide notice to an army in the region.

It took Keogh, in charge of the pack train, an hour and a half to get the mules across the swampy bottoms of Mud Creek in the darkness, the column held impatiently on the other bank while he tried to curse and pound efficiency into the mules and the packers. He was greatly disturbed by the confusion and by the vagaries of the loose pack animals wandering in the dark. Benteen went back to help a little, advising Keogh to take it easier, that nothing short of a howling, arrow-pricking Indian charge could run off one of those mules. Some of the badly tied packs might slip down and be left behind, but these could be recovered at daylight.

When Varnum came in from a long scout, the big man stiff and worn for sleep, Custer told him that the Crows spoke of a high hill about twenty miles ahead, with a pocket on the slope, one big enough to hide the scout horses. The point, called the Crow's Nest, was on the divide.

"At daylight one can see by the rising of the smoke whether there are Indians on the Little Bighorn or not."

But for this important scout the colonel wanted an intelligent white man to go along to verify what the Indians saw and send word back to him.

Wearily the lieutenant nodded to himself. "I guess that means me . . .," he said, and climbed into the saddle. He selected the quiet, reserved, and experienced Charley Reynolds, even though his infected trigger hand was still swollen, and added Bouyer and several Crows, all men who knew the country, every moccasin track of it.

Through Girard the commander explained his instructions to several Rees he was sending along as a further check on the Crow scouts, who were, after all, Gibbon's men, not Custer's of solid acquaintance and promise, as the Rees of the Missouri River were.

Finally the column began to move, and although the stars hung clear and bright, the dust rose in a gray, furry haze that shut away even the dark masses of the troops as they turned from the pleasant minty bottoms of the Rosebud and headed westward, up along the breaks of Davis Creek. The sections of the command had a difficult time keeping anywhere near each other, let alone following the troop ahead. The jingle and creak of equipment and the snort of the horses helped. Hoofs, soft in the dust, sounded louder on the stretches of baked earth where their shoes struck sparks from the flinty gravel. Gradually the dust lessened on the rising trail to the Little Bighorn and communication became easier as the night turned toward the morning of June 25.

»▶ »▶ »▶ »▶ »▶ »▶ »▶ »▶

2 OVER
THE DIVIDE

★ ★ ★ ★ ★ ★ ★ ★

George Armstrong Custer led his 7th U. S. Cavalry through
the pitch dark, Girard, the former trader and now the official
Ree interpreter, riding beside him. Half Yellow Face, leader
of the Crow scouts, knew every break and ridge and washout
over the Little Bighorn, but he kept close, too, sometimes
barely keeping up even with the commander's strong horse, although he was supposed to be out ahead, picking the trail.

The clouded night hung low and unbroken, the occasional
flicker of lightning low in the northwest too far away to light
even a silhouette of the rising hills called Wolf Mountains.
Behind Custer the stinging alkali dust was riffled now and then
by a light breeze that sprang up like a bird fleeing before a
coyote. Then the little wind was gone, the temporary billowing
of the dust cloud sensed more by the nostrils, even through
a bandanna drawn up over the nose, than by the eye in the
darkness. The horses within the troops still had trouble following each other; the van of the units was sometimes forced to
halt and listen, hand cupped to the ear, to catch the direction

of those ahead, perhaps guided by the signaling taps of a tin cup or a canteen against the saddle as the command felt its way. Now and then a section might be caught in a little box canyon or snakehead draw, the men compelled to turn upon themselves to get out, and yet always the thrust was upward toward the divide, awkwardly but with determination toward the divide between the Rosebud and the Wolf Mountains. Sometimes Custer himself was stopped while one of the Indians got off to feel the earth for a turn or swerve in the worn lodge-pole trail they tried to follow around bluff side or canyon. Even with all the caution, now and then some weary horse stumbled on a washed-out buffalo trail, stepped into a badger hole, or lost its footing at a cut bank, to struggle and fall. The rider, perhaps thrown out of a saddle sleep, awoke, cursing and shouting to stop those immediately behind, the horse, up, grabbing hungrily for a mouthful of grass or weed through bitted teeth.

Keogh, with Lieutenant Mathey of the pack string, was far back along the trail, struggling, with the mules—naturally sharper-eyed and surer-footed than horses, but hungry enough to stray badly now—and the packers were cursed out as an un-skilled, shiftless lot. Each time they were gathered up, the mules brayed their lonely desolation, their weary protest usually an-swered from up ahead, where Mark Kellogg rode—the repeated brayings surely the signal of an approaching army to any hostile Indian within five miles. Even without the noisy outbreaks, any Sioux could feel the cadence of so many hoofs with his palm, his fingertips, laid to the bare earth. Not that there was danger of a night attack from the Sioux. Night fighting was considered unlucky, with the dew-softened moccasins vulnerable to any rosethorn and cactus, the wet bowstrings stretched so they re-fused to send the arrow against an enemy. But dawn would come, the time of Indian ambush and attack—and where the

Sioux chose. Still no one dared suggest a halt to Custer, although he knew from his scouts, white and Crow, that he could not hope to find a protected bivouac beyond the divide, no safe place to hide a mounted regiment until the next night, while the Indian camp was located and the troops made ready to meet General Terry.

It was a slow, weary march, and several times one troop commander or another dropped back to talk the situation over, or to keep himself awake by recalling that day after tomorrow, the 27th, the Democratic Convention* opened at St. Louis, the nominee, with all the scandals around Grant, given the first good chance against the Republicans since the Civil War. How would such a victory affect the officers stationed over the South, and in the Plains Army, and the whole Indian extermination policy—all sponsored by Republican administrations? What of the career men in the army?

Out—practically everybody out—most thought, except those who knew of Custer's optimistic prediction to his Ree scouts. He would surely try.

So a painful eight or ten miles were covered, the horses and men both worn, the scouts who had been in the saddle most of the nights up the Rosebud sleeping on their horses while they could. Then, as the grayness began to creep into the clouds overhead, the movement in the van suddenly stopped, the troops spreading out as they came up to a flattish bottom under a bluff that was still more to be felt than seen in the darkness. The thirsty horses broke for the thin thread and the stinking pools

* In a box of Custer battle souvenirs loaned by the Sioux of Pine Ridge Reservation, S. Dak., to John Colhoff, the author's interpreter with the old buffalo hunters, to show her, was an unidentifiable fragment of notebook with the following entry: "June 24. The political discussions are still going on. Kellog [sic] gets in a real sweat as do some others. There's a lot hangs on what's done at the conventions. St. Louis will tell whether the army is cut, rumors report."

of upper Davis Creek; but they snorted and threw themselves back from the water that was so alkaline that the coffee from it was undrinkable.

Most of the stock was left under saddle, but some of the older troopers slipped them off for a few minutes, rubbing the sweat-scalded backs of their horses with twists of weeds, and reluctantly set the leather back into place, leaving the cinches loose, the bits out of the mouths so the tethered animals could eat the little grass available. The recruits and young Boston Custer and Autie Reed tried to ease their own saddle gall and the sting of the alkali, while the hardened campaigners sprawled on the ground, snoring the dust from their nostrils.

But Colonel Custer had other concerns than the gray coffee or even the weary horses and men. He was anxious for news from his scouts. With his brother, Captain Tom, and Adjutant Cooke he waited while the younger members of the Custer family slept, for all their excitement.

Scouts had gone out in several groups from the last camp on the Rosebud, in addition to Bob Tail Bull away wolfing alone for sign since the noon before. The Crows with Lieutenant Varnum knew all this country and led him directly toward the high lookout butte called the Crow's Nest. The party stopped twice to smoke. The Indians shielded the small point of light in the bowl and made some quiet talk among themselves. There was uneasiness in those who had been out ahead to examine the warming trail of the Sioux.

"The Indians are very, very many," Varnum was told, but with the low, flat tone used to one known to be totally deaf, whether deaf to their warning by his choice or that of his commander. They were embarrassed by this because they liked the big-nosed, broad-mustached young officer. He had endurance, and was not working to get himself ahead.

"Yes, there are very many Sioux," the Rees agreed, making the signs. "All the Tetons from all over . . ."

When the pipe was put away, the scouts headed up the rises toward the lookout butte. At about two-thirty they stopped in the pocket the Crows had described, and unsaddled. Varnum was worn out from his scouting since yesterday, thirty-six hours without sleep or even rest, on top of almost continuous work since they left the Yellowstone. He stretched his long body awkwardly in the darkness for a little sleep while two scouts, including Hairy Moccasin, the smallest and most alert of the Crows, climbed to the peak of the Nest.

After an hour or so there was an owl's hoot from up on the point, vaguely touched on the east by the coming dawn. It wasn't a loud hoot, but clear, and in meaning too, apparently, for the Rees around Varnum began to sing their death songs until silenced by the scouts coming down from the lookout. Through signs the two Crows reported Sioux tipis ahead. Varnum, awakened by the voice of Hairy Moccasin, saw him standing among the scattering of dark trees against the gray sky and went to lead the clamber up to the point. On either side the earth fell away; the slopes of gray rock, sage, and sparse grass were dotted with the green-black of cedar and jack pines coming out of the foggy morning haze. Far down the eastern slopes there was the bluer drift of smoke from the regimental fires creeping up across the daybreak.

"Does Custer think the Sioux have white-man eyes?" the Crows demanded sourly, their thin lips curling in contempt.

Northwestward the land descended in broken steps to a shallow valley still in darkness but where, the scouts said, they could see tipi smoke and horse herds. Varnum pulled the spyglass out long and looked, then watched the Indian faces as the light grew, showing the timber-shielded Little Bighorn snake across the prairie and dip down behind a row of bluffs. One by one the

Indians exclaimed and pointed northward, to where the mist seemed denser, darker, and under it the sense rather than the sight of movement, a confused and widespread stirring. The Crows spoke among themselves in awed voices.

Charley Reynolds took a look through the glass and remarked mildly, "That's the biggest pony herd any man ever saw together . . ."

"Biggest camp, like every summer," Bouyer amended, with French emphasis and Indian directness. "Far too big."

As the light spread out of the east through the cover of clouds, Varnum strained his eyes, blurred and bloodshot from the seventy hours of dusty scouting, first with Reno, now Custer.

"Look for nest of worms," Mitch Bouyer suggested. "Big pony herd far off look like tangles of fish worms."

Still Varnum saw nothing, but he realized from the excitement that the others did and knew that their findings would be sound. He wrote a note to Custer saying that the Sioux had been located, and started Red Star, a young Ree, off with the message a little after four-thirty. The Indian stopped to tie up his horse's tail in the sign of war and headed down toward the regiment, Bull going along with the verbal report for double security but lagging because his horse was worn and weak from travel and too little feed and water.

Up on the Crow's Nest, Varnum and his scouts saw six enemy Indians* leave cover near the hill. Four rode off into the sparse clumps of timber, but two slipped down a dry coulee that cut in ahead of Red Star and Bull. At first Varnum thought of trying to overtake them, kill them; but firing shots now, with the enemy apparently very close, would betray the whole regiment, destroy the last hope of a surprise or even a close approach.

* Little Wolf's Cheyennes, on their way from Red Cloud to the summer conference.

Motioning for silence, he listened, a cupped hand to his ear, the glass searching for a blue puff of black powder smoke; but there was no gunshot, and arrows seemed unlikely against the carbines of the scouts if Bull's horse didn't drop out entirely.

Apparently the couriers weren't discovered at all, and when Red Star came in sight of the blue-clad sentries he gave the whoop of success and rode his horse zigzag back and forth on a rise, meaning, "Enemy found!"

Several Rees hurried out to meet him, escort him into camp just as the early sun found a rift in the clouds. Bloody Knife and Stabbed, the holy man, hurried up with praise that Red Star had been chosen to carry the message. There was a pipe to be smoked, and a little thanking ceremony to be made at this honor to their young man. In the meantime another party of scouts came in and had to hear the news.

Ah-h, then probably everybody would have to hurry out for more spying on the Sioux, the leader remarked thoughtfully.

"Yes, but let us get breakfast first," someone said. "If we must go to the happy hunting ground of the missionaries we should go on a full belly."

But even with this nearness to a fight, some of the scouts just in were too worn to eat, and the others swallowed their food as fast as they could, their eyes on the little knoll where Custer's tent stood.

Most of the soldiers were still stretched on the ground, asleep, but the officers were moving around and saw Red Star return. When Custer heard about this he didn't wait for the news to be brought to him in the formal Indian way but came with Girard to interpret, Captain Tom Custer along and Mark Kellogg edging up. The colonel settled to his usual posture, leaning on his left knee, and made signs to Red Star, asking about the Sioux. The young Indian was still cooling his tin cup of coffee, and answered by drawing Varnum's note from his pocket. Then he took cautious sips of the cup while Custer read of the scout findings at the Crow's Nest, his bristly, sun-raw face growing jubilant.

By now, more Indians had come to squat in a sort of circle before Custer; the dozen pairs of expressionless eyes on him apparently pushed him to a feeble attempt at humor. By signs to Bloody Knife he pretended it was not the Indians who were afraid but his brother, Captain Tom.

"His heart flutters with fear at this news of the Sioux," he said. "When we have whipped them, he will be a man."

This seemed puzzling foolishness even after Girard tried to interpret it. Custer was only half listening, his weary face lined, his eyes focused far away. Something in Bloody Knife's serious reply jerked the colonel's attention back to the circle of Indians.

"What's that he's saying?" he demanded.

Slowly, formally, Bloody Knife rose to repeat his words, taking advantage of his position as favorite scout of the commander. "There are too many Sioux over there," he said. "All the Tetons come together. It would take many days to kill them all."

Custer laughed at the brown faces about him, suddenly elated once more by the prospect of an early encounter and a victory that would astonish these Indians who had never seen a real general in action.

"Oh," he said casually, "I guess we'll get through with them in one day."

He said it confidently as he had told a luncheon given for him by an associate of Jay Gould that his 7th Cavalry could whip all the Indians on the Plains. And it was a good time now for a military victory, only nine days to the Fourth of July and the national centennial, a hundred years since the Declaration of Independence was signed. It was an excellent time to defeat the warring Sioux, and today the best time of all, with the Democratic Convention opening the day after tomorrow, and

James Gordon Bennett of the New York *Herald* or his lieuten-
ants surely prepared to stampede the convention for his friend,
General George Armstrong Custer. Or Jay Gould of the New
York *World* and the western railroads might be as effective.
Victory now would leave two days and three nights to get the
news to the telegraph office and to the Convention at St. Louis.
Charley Reynolds, who had carried Custer's news of gold in the
Black Hills out to the world, could reach the telegraph office at
Bozeman in less than two days with a terse account that Custer
would write. There would be additional messengers for insur-
ance, Herendeen and others, each taking a different route,
Bouyer to spur down to the telegraph at the North Platte River,
with Custer himself probably making the run to the Missouri
River—Custer for this run and Mark Kellogg. A victory telegram
read at the Convention the morning of the 28th would do it,
so he must succeed by sundown this evening, even if the defeated were only a small camp, only the "half a dozen Sioux
lodges" that he had told the Ree scouts would make him the
Great Father, the President.

In his elation Custer leaped to the first horse he reached, and
rode at a gallop bareback through the command, the fringes of
his buckskin sleeves flapping as he shouted orders to prepare
for marching at eight. Behind the dust of his running horse the
officers hurried into knots of three and four for a hasty breakfast and some guarded talk about the colonel's excitement and
what lay ahead as they tried to wet down their dry food with the
alkalied coffee or the dregs from stale canteens. The horses were
still without water, a few trying to break away, many with heads
down, their tongues so parched that the oats they tried to eat
fell dry from their muzzles. By now the news had spread
through the troopers: the Sioux camp was seen on the Little
Bighorn, twelve–fifteen miles beyond the divide that lay before
them.

A little after eight, without orders or bugle call, the advance troop began to move behind Custer, in a clean gray-blue shirt now, and buckskin suit and his broad whitish hat. The rest of the command followed, one troop after another, the pack train still in the rear and lagging. For about two hours and a half the regiment crawled up the hostile slopes, many of the rolling foothills topped by bald knobs of gray rock under the pale sky. They moved slowly through the lower cuts and passes, parallel to the deep Indian trail, but trying to keep to sod or stone to decrease the dust that was so trying to the thirsty stock and the burned-lipped men. Still it plumed upward where the regiment had passed, a war signal to even a far-off Indian. The windrows of thin clouds cut off the direct scorch of the sun but not the heat, so the men sweltered under the sultry, whitish sky, the horses wild to reach some creek, or plodding in weariness and exhaustion. After the march of about ten miles to the foot of the Crow's Nest, the command was hidden as well as possible to wait until the colonel returned from his ride ahead to the lookout.

When Custer first climbed the peak of the Crow's Nest, Charley Reynolds pointed to a spot for observation. With field glasses to his eyes, the colonel stared a long time into the bluish haze that was creeping over much of the lightly shadowed heights and hollows. He looked and said he was unable to distinguish what others called lodge smoke or even the movement of the enormous pony herds, probably on the way to water or returning to the grassy hills beyond the Little Bighorn. Despite the certainty of the scouts and the efforts of Reynolds and Bouyer, Custer insisted he saw nothing.

"I've been on the Plains a good many years," he reminded them. "My eyesight is as good as yours and I can't see anything that looks like Indian ponies."

Charley Reynolds held his usual silence but Bouyer's black-bearded face grew furious. "If you don't find more Indians in that valley than you ever saw before, you can string me up."

"All right, all right; what good would it do to hang you?" the colonel exclaimed impatiently.

Perhaps to bolster his public contention that there was no Indian village ahead, Custer claimed no hostiles could have seen the command. He rejected Varnum's report of the Indians at the foot of the hill earlier and that they must have noticed the fresh tracks of shod horses, at least of his and the white scouts'. Surely they saw the dust spreading back where the column had marched.

Curiously, the commander seemed opposed to Half Yellow Face's urging for an immediate attack, saying he planned to wait for night, although no one around believed this. Mitch Bouyer, who had worked with the trader whisky wagons among the Sioux and Northern Cheyenne camps for years, knew their power and the size of the Teton summer councils that were driven from Bear Butte by the miners. He had one suggestion for Custer: "Get your outfit out of the country as fast as your played-out horses can carry you."

There was no reply to this, barely an acknowledgment. Not that Bouyer could have expected a response to any protesting voice, or voices, all plainly less than the shake of a cottonwood leaf in the wind today.

The scouts talked gravely among themselves, glancing off toward the Little Bighorn and then toward their homes, none of them convinced that Custer really intended to hide out to dusk, most of them certain that he would not hold back. True, men like Reynolds and the older officers of the 7th knew that Custer's one successful encounter with Indians was his attack on the Southern Cheyennes on the Washita. That had started with a charge out of a frosty winter dawn, with Chief Black Kettle just back from a talk with their agent, Colonel Hazen, to the camp on their reservation, supposedly safe. There, as at Sand Creek, the Cheyennes were shot down running from their winter sleeping robes and as they were last March when Crook's force struck them in the Powder River country.

The Sioux had managed to elude all such early-morning attacks. Their one real defeat by the army was in daylight during the old peace days, before the tribe realized they were in a war. Harney had approached them under the pretext of friendly counciling and when Little Thunder's band was surrounded, the guns and cannons began to boom.

As Reynolds, Bouyer, and the Crows knew, and particularly Bloody Knife and his Rees, the Sioux over there on the Little Bighorn were not a single band under a peace chief but practically all the Tetons of war age; their chiefs, war leaders like Sitting Bull, Crazy Horse, Big Road, Crow King, and Gall. Besides, Custer had no cannon like Harney—not even the Gatling guns that Brisbin had offered, even urged.

Down in the ravine the hidden regiment was close-packed; men and horses jammed together, airless and burning hot, mouths parched, tongues swelling. While loosening his girth, Sergeant Curtis discovered he had lost some clothing from his saddle roll on the awkward uphill march. He got permission from Captain Yates to slip down along the trail to search for it but came galloping back, spurring as fast as his horse could run. He had found a box of hardtack dropped from one of the mule packs with several Indians squatting around it. They fled to their horses and headed toward the Little Bighorn when they saw him come—all but one, who stopped off on a ridge out of carbine range, but with a rifle glinting across his saddle. He waited, looking, certainly understanding, what the deep, fresh trail of shod horses meant, the trail of many, many iron-hoofed cavalry horses barely past, even if he and the others hadn't actually seen the dusty regiment and the long train of mule packs that surely contained ammunition, coffee and sugar, too— but best of all, the long-forbidden ammunition.

Custer was told this when he came riding down a draw from the Crow's Nest to gather his officers around him. He reported what they all knew: that the Crow scouts insisted they could see tipi tops on the favored campground of the Sioux, the Little Bighorn. Lots of ponies too, and dust and smoke. But he had looked through the binoculars himself, and said that he saw nothing and did not believe anyone else did either. How many of the men standing before him believed that his words were sincere could only be guessed, but certainly they all understood his agitation, the burning of his dust-reddened eyes, the stutter trapping his excited tongue.

The Ree scouts had stepped aside from the scouting here and from the lookout because it was Crow country. But now there was to be shooting, and so they prepared as well as they could against their ancient and most relentless enemy, the Sioux—this time in overwhelming numbers, fresh warriors on fast war horses, while the Rees were very few, mostly on thirsting and worn-out ponies.

After awhile Custer came to them and said if they would not fight they might at least hurry ahead fast to take all the Sioux horses that they could. At this order Stabbed, the medicine man, rode out before his tribesmen and, turning his horse back and forth, exhorted the young men to keep up their courage. The battle today would be a hard one, and many of his brothers were raw and inexperienced, going into their first real shooting. Then the medicine man dismounted and, opening his large painted bag, took out bits of clay to rub between his spit-moistened palms, singing a little, a thin, high song for power against the enemy. Finally he called the young men to him so he could rub the good medicine on their bodies against arrow, spear, and bullet.

The scouts lined up with none of the joy and anticipation usual before a good fight with horses and other booty possible, not even in the most eager youths. There was nothing now except Stabbed's silent painting with the clay and the plaintive song of one of the Rees off on a hillside, his arms lifted to the sky. One man after another the scouts stepped up to the medicine man, holding their dusty, faded shirts away from their brown bodies for the daubing with clay, even the older men whose chests were scarred from warrior ordeals.

Bloody Knife, in command of the Rees, asked to make a little talk with Custer. Through Girard he recalled that once before he had nearly touched death while with the colonel, on the Black Hills expedition. The wagons had got stuck and because Long Hair* thought it was Bloody Knife's fault, he aimed a carbine shot at him.

"Later I asked you to come back," Custer reminded the scout, "and apologized."

"Ahh, that is true, and I said it was not a good thing, this that you had done. If I, too, had been possessed by madness, you would not have seen another day."

The Rees murmured in concern, many hearing of this shooting at their head man for the first time. But Custer paid no attention to them, apparently concerned with deep plans and preparations. Bloody Knife spoke again, as out of some inner compulsion, and very gravely. "I am going home today, not the way we came, but in spirit, home to my people."

The commander of the 7th Cavalry smiled a little, his burned

* Common Indian name for Custer before he—along with the rest of the regiment—was ordered to cut his hair in 1876.

lips thin under the red stubbling, but his mind was plainly too engrossed for much show of scorn or even concern for this fear of a bunch of wild Indians, or for a repetition of the promise to take Bloody Knife to Washington when he had made himself the Great Father.

After a fireless breakfast of raw bacon, hardtack, and stale canteen water the command moved. The heat of the coming noonday lay over the high ground of the divide as the command started up the last slope. On an open place where grouse panted behind the scattered clumps of weed, Custer halted the regiment and ordered each troop commander to send a noncommissioned officer and six enlisted men back to take charge of the pack mules of his unit and help Lieutenant Mathey protect the train. Then the colonel turned to the formation of his column for attack, announcing that the first troop commander to report his pack detail completed and each trooper carrying the proper 100 rounds of carbine ammunition and 24 rounds for the pistol would receive the advance position.

There was no telling the commander's preference for this important and honored place but Benteen had his men right there behind him and it was impossible not to volunteer without implying that the officers of H Troop were a lax and unsoldierly lot, so he spoke up, certain that his unit was in order as a matter of course.

Custer accepted the salute. "Then, Colonel Benteen," he said, his stammer noticeably increased by the agitation of the day, "you have the advance, sir."

McDougall, the last commander to report ready, was detailed to help guard the pack train as penalty. With the regiment standing in columns of fours, Custer notified Benteen to move his troop to the right, but before long he galloped up to say that the captain's pace was too fast. Taking the front himself, Custer

led the 7th out across the heavily traveled saddle of the divide
and toward the Little Bighorn, twelve–thirteen miles away, the
Crows said. If anyone recalled that Custer was to locate the
Indians, scout their numbers and movements to prevent any
slip southward to Crook's department, with an outranking for
Custer if he met the general's force, apparently none spoke of it.
Or that tomorrow evening or the next day they were to meet
General Terry on the Little Bighorn with the information
gleaned in the scouting. Certainly none would have dared men-
tion such ideas, or remind the commander that Gibbon's last
advice as the regiment started was, "Now, Custer, don't be
greedy."

After awhile the column was halted and dismounted for a
breather. Custer, with his adjutant, drew off a few yards in the
advance, just out of earshot, to plan and make notes on what
looked like a memo book or scratch pad. After fifteen minutes or
so, Cooke came galloping back to Benteen with orders from the
commander. He was to mount D and K Troops in addition to
his H outfit and proceed left at an angle of about 45 degrees
west-southwest to the line of march, going to a ridge of high
bluffs about two miles off, and apparently on and on. He was
to keep a well-mounted officer and ten men in advance, be prepared to pitch into any Indians he could find, and notify the
commander at once of any encounter.

With Lieutenant Gibson and ten troopers in the van, but
with no Indian scouts—not one man with Benteen who knew
anything of the country—the captain led out toward the rough
breaks of the Wolf Mountains, off to the left. He moved
through foothills from one steep ridge to the next, knowing
from his years on the Plains that the trail he left behind was of
eight, ten, or even fifteen thousand Indians who must be on the

Little Bighorn—surely where the scouts saw the lodges and the great pony herds. Yet, if any Sioux were ahead of him, even a thousand or two, his orders were to "pitch into" them with his force of 120 men. But with no turn-off on the trail, no sign of hoof or moccasin anywhere, it seemed he was sent chasing a bunghole bugle, a wind trumpet, sent on a fool's errand like any green looey come west.

As he passed Reno, still with no command, the major called to Benteen, asking where he was going.

"To those hills over there, to drive everything before me," the captain replied sourly as he led Weir and Godfrey and the three troops off across the dry canyons.

About a mile on, Custer's chief trumpeter was sent to Benteen with the commander's compliments and additional orders. If nothing was visible from the far ridge, he was to go to the next. Later the sergeant-major of the regiment galloped away to Benteen with further instructions from Custer: go to the next line of bluffs and on to the valley beyond, and, by implication, on and on. The orders, altogether, were almost like a sort of lopping-off of his men, as a branch is cut from the tree, from the living fluid of the trunk.

In the meantime Custer had made further division of his command and sent the bearded Cooke on to Major Reno. "The general directs you to take specific command of Companies A, G, and M."

When there was no clarification, no order of specific disposition, purpose, or objective, Reno asked, "Is that all?"

"Yes," the big adjutant replied and, wheeling his horse, was gone.

So now the 7th Cavalry was once more organized into battalions. Reno had made such division at Fort Lincoln while Custer was away in Washington; but when the commander returned, he immediately divided the regiment into wings, Reno in command of the right, Benteen the left; and then at the Yellowstone camp he had reduced it to individual troops under his own firm hand. Now, facing a fight, Custer returned to the battalion unit—three instead of Reno's four.

Varnum and Hare pushed the protesting and apprehensive scouts out ahead of the two columns hurrying along the Indian trail, but never got them far beyond the guns of the troopers. Boston Custer, Autie Reed, and Mark Kellogg rode together, close to the commander. Like the troops, they were silent now. The bluffs with stunted evergreens shut out all sign of the Little Bighorn and its own protecting ridges, while far behind somewhere McDougall was trying to hurry the pack mules along.

From the dry head of Ash Creek the evergreens began to thin and vanish, but the Indian trail clung to the narrow valley that led far off to the river. There were several cracked and dried mudholes, and then swampy spots from seepages gone dry with summer, one with the warning stink of some animal caught in the bogs—a buffalo; only the balding head out above the dried scum over the mud, the eyesockets a writhing of worms. The water-desperate horses tried to plunge into the bogs, too, but were held back with bit and quirt and spur.

While Custer pushed on along the right side of the shallow canyon, Reno started down the left, Lieutenant Hodgson galloping back to instruct each company to ride a little to the side of the one ahead, to keep the betraying dust down. Both battalions moved parallel to the wide Indian trail that had been increased once more by a branch, this one apparently from higher up the Rosebud—a war trail, with no tracks of lodgepoles, no colts, no sign of lagging old mares.

Suddenly the advance scouts slowed, pointing ahead openly,

not as to an enemy discovered but with more excitement than for a deer or even a buffalo. It was a tipi, painted and alone, standing out on a widened little bottom of Ash Creek, dried now, but with water in the spring.

Custer stopped, spoke to Girard, who signaled to the Rees, calling out, "The chief says for you to run!"

At this Strikes Two gave a war whoop and charged in, the first to count coup on the tipi, his riding whip popping against the dry hides. Young Hawk, just behind, jumped from his horse and with the long knife from his belt slashed the lodge open from top to the ground. Inside was a dead smell from the scaffold with a body* wrapped in a beaded buffalo robe, a feathered shield with bow and quiver, and a pipe and fire bag beside him; meat and even a wooden bowl of soup lay at the foot of the posts. Although it was plain that part of the Sioux had camped here very recently, no one of Custer's command seemed particularly interested that the Indian had died of bullets, of war wounds. None could know that eight days ago warriors from here had gone to attack Crook on the Rosebud, not far above Custer's turn-off at Davis Creek; but others besides the scouts must have discovered this, at least recognized the new trail coming in from the left as that of a very big and triumphant war party, multiplying the danger ahead at the river.

Reno stood high in his stirrups looking out over the rising ground and outcroppings of striated, weathered old sandstone on both sides of the little valley. As he expected, there were Indians, off some distance, watching; twenty men, perhaps even forty or a hundred hidden in an ambush; those in sight sitting on their horses with no sign of surprise or alarm at all these soldiers. They were just out of carbine range, as though inviting

* Old She Bear, wounded in the Rosebud fight, June 17. He was the brother of Circling or Turning Bear.

pursuit, but when the major and his scouts followed them a short distance, they still kept just ahead, the hoofs of their ponies spurting up dust.

By the time Reno returned to his troops, some of the scouts had whipped back to Custer, who ordered them to follow the fleeing Sioux, attack them. Silently the Indians refused, so now here was the showdown that all had felt coming from the first alarmed report that the Rees had made, far back down the Rosebud.

"We are scouts, to find the Sioux, not to fight them," Girard and Bouyer finally interpreted for the Indians, Crows as well as Rees.

Custer snorted, stammering in his anger. "Take the guns and horses from them!" he shouted. "Let them run home to their women!"

The scouts still refused to move, silent again under his common insult to their women. They looked away, around the closed-in horizon, finally speaking among themselves of the scattered command: Benteen far out of sight in the broken country, Reno up ahead. They gathered in little knots, some with army horses turning them over to the stable sergeants and mounting their own ponies, determined to hold to Custer's earlier promise that they need not fight, just take all the Sioux horses they could. So together they returned to Varnum and Hare.

Custer sent Adjutant Cooke loping after Reno with the news —the admission that there was a Sioux village at the river, said to be not more than two miles away, and that the Indians were running away.

"General Custer directs you to take as rapid a gait as you think prudent and charge the village, and you will be supported by the whole outfit."

The excitement of the men close enough to overhear the

order ran through the whole three companies, weary as they were, they and their horses. Lieutenant Wallace, recorder of the regiment, fell in beside Reno's adjutant, Lieutenant Hodgson, both reining close behind the major as he led off down the left side of the dry run that became the southwest side of Ash Creek. Reno was on the wide, worn lodge trail that followed the curves of the bed of sand and stagnant pools, with Custer's force off to the right, the pack train far behind somewhere, only a faint rising of dust any indication that it existed at all. There was no sign of Benteen, marching at the 45-degree angle leftward, no telling where in the rough breaks of the Wolf Mountains, or some valley beyond.

And ahead of Reno, through a cut, the men saw the tops of a few trees—the Little Bighorn. A cheer broke from them as they spurred ahead.

3 RENO
ON THE
BOTTOMS

★ ★ ★ ★ ★ ★ ★ ★ ★

During his nine years out of West Point, Major Marcus Reno had been in the dragoons, the cavalry, and the Freedman's Bureau, served as acting inspector-general, on such boards as Retirement and Small Arms, and commanded Fort Totten and Fort Lincoln. His Civil War record was excellent, with several brevets, including a commission as Brevet Brigadier General of the U. S. Volunteers in 1865. It was perhaps characteristic of the man that neither he nor anyone else often thought of him as a general or very often called him that.

Now the afternoon of June 25, sometime between one o'clock and two-thirty—a difference between a guess at the sun's height and the watches running on the Chicago time of Fort Lincoln— Major Reno looked back over his dusty, march-worn battalion standing in twos. He drew his broad hat to his black eyebrows, turned his stocky body in the saddle, and struck out at a gallop down the drying creek for the Little Bighorn, leading his force of 112 men and the scouts, promised by Custer they need not fight.

The major soon slowed his pace to avoid winding the tired horses. By then Adjutant Cooke and Captain Keogh had crossed over from Custer's battalion to ride beside him for a while, their purpose not clearly defined. In the meantime Custer was slacking his pace too, lengthening the distance between the two columns. He had the young Crow breed, Curly, and Mitch Bouyer to scout for him, both men familiar with every break and canyon in the region. Most of the other Indian scouts had been ordered to Reno's force with the interpreters Girard, Dorman, and Billy Jackson, as well as Charley Reynolds and Terry's courier Herendeen, never sent back to the general. Even Bloody Knife, Custer's man, was with Reno in a sort of banishment. From the start the Indians had lagged, either deliberately or because their ponies were gaunt and worn by the long, thirsty travel and the lack of feed. Some trooper stock, too, fell back in spite of raw and bleeding sides roweled by spurs.

As the Indian trail crossed over to the wider bottoms on the left side of the little creek, Reno drew his horse in to keep the column closer together. By now all sight of Custer's men was cut off by an intervening tongue of rise; but ahead of the major there were glimpses of brush and trees, a glint of water too, and a great wall of dust climbing to the cloud-streaked sky of the northwest. Then suddenly the valley of the Little Bighorn opened before them, the dry, rolling, sunburned bottoms left of the stream, with a rimming of higher ground beyond, while on Reno's side, below the trail ford and the mouth of Ash Creek, steep, yellowish bluffs, gashed and torn, rose abruptly from the river bank and followed it, apparently for two–three miles.

As the smell of water reached the horses many that had lagged became wild, rearing, trying to run, those of the recruits breaking unchecked for the river, with officers spurring after them, shouting orders and caution.

"Don't let the horses jump off the high bank!"

"Don't let them bloat themselves, make themselves so logy they can't run . . ."

"Don't let them founder, die right under the saddle!"

But even so, many took the bit and plunged into the stream, throwing water high, thrusting their burned muzzles deep into the current as they drank frantically, refusing to break out of the river for whip, spur, or profanity. The men drank as thirstily, many too much, in spite of all the warnings. Then the canteens were gathered up.

"Fill them to the top! We're going into a hard fight!" the sergeants warned.

In the meantime the Rees had stopped on the far bank, refusing to cross at all. They listened, sullen and unmoved, to Lieutenant Varnum's exhortations. A few edged their horses off to the side and vanished into the breaks.

By now there was more dust down the tree-patched snake bends of the Little Bighorn indicating where the great Sioux village probably stood, and that warriors, many warriors, must be running their horses back and forth for that second wind that would carry them through a good fight. Besides, a great dust shielded not only their activities and numbers but any ambush planned.

Reno glanced anxiously back for Custer, for his support, as he worked the command across the Little Bighorn and out upon the bottoms. Cooke and Keogh were all that was visible of the Custer battalion. They sat their horses, watching awhile. Then they shouted "Good luck!" and turned back.

Girard, coming down from a bluff overlooking the river, called out that there were many Indians under the stirring dust and many, many more were whipping up along the bank from farther down. He hailed Cooke and explained what he had seen. The adjutant listened, promised to report it all to Custer, and set off rapidly back up the creek trail.

While Reno labored to form his battalion into some order, Varnum was still on the far side of the river, frantically shouting his contempt against the stubborn Rees, who understood few of the words but all of the meaning. When Girard returned, the lieutenant called to the interpreter, who hurried in to lash the Rees in their own tongue, roaring like a haranguing war chief. Finally a dozen or so did cross the river with him and Varnum, Hare, Charley Reynolds, and Isaiah Dorman, the Negro interpreter, but reluctantly looking back to Stabbed, their medicine man, rooted on the far side.

In the meantime the bellowing noncoms had reduced some of the confusion. With the girths tightened, the troopers forced their dripping horses into place, perhaps rearing and bucking, or plodding, head down. The command, finally solidified into troops, faced a stretch of about two miles that was mostly prairie-dog town and empty sage-dotted second bottom to a thumb of brush and timber extending leftward from the river bank. It was beyond this protection that the cloud of dust lifted upward, with faint whoops now and then carrying against the light cross-wind. Reno looked back over his water-spattered column to the ford that was still empty, even the dust of Cooke and Keogh's departure thinned away, and no sign of a dashing figure in a wide white hat leading five troops to the fight. Anxiously, Reno beckoned his striker, McIlhargy, of Keogh's Company I, which had served under the major on the Canadian border survey back in 1873–74. Supplying the private with one of the stronger horses left, Reno sent the shrewd, resourceful man to hurry to Custer, probably off somewhere behind the line of steep bluffs across the river by now and with no ford for miles down the stream, as both Curly and Bouyer must have told the colonel.

It was an urgent call for the promised support. "I have everything ahead of me and the enemy is strong."

The major turned in the saddle to watch the courier cross the river and vanish around the bluff up the little creek. Then, rising in his stirrups, he ordered two of his companies forward, the third, under Lieutenant McIntosh, to remain back in reserve. Spurring ahead, Reno led the charge down the dry bottoms, the men in fours behind him, the horses jumping the prairie-dog holes, shying at the audacious barks, and, beyond the dog town, stirring up the smell of sage in the hot, still air. After a mile or so, the lathering, the laboring of his horses and the sign of increasing force at his front decided Reno to form the two companies into line, the reluctant scouts under Varnum well off to the left, toward the rising ground, with Girard, Herendeen, Reynolds, and the other civilians between them and the troops but not taking much part either, beyond firing a long shot or two, watching the fight start. When the Indians began to shoot, the scouts rode down to the patch of timber extending out of the snake bends of the river and left the horses near a natural clearing in the center. From there they scattered out casually through brush and weeds to see where the encounter was going and then slipped back, one after the other, for their horses.

By now the Sioux ahead were firing more frequently and whooping louder as they charged up, stripped to breechclout, more and more of them painted for war, but still breaking easily into retreat—too easily, as the old campaigners on the bottoms knew. Plainly, they outnumbered Reno several times over, knew their terrain, hidden by the dust, and had their village, their

women and children, to defend. Yet they made no real effort to
check the advancing troops. It could only mean an ambush.

With still no support from beyond the river, Reno sent Adjutant Hodgson to bring up Lieutenant McIntosh and his G Troop.
In the meantime he started Mitchell, his cook, also from
Keogh's Company I, with a more urgent message to Custer.
From the bottoms Girard thought he caught a glimpse of the
Gray Horse Troop riding hard along the ridges beyond the
river, but perhaps it was only the nine Rees who had remained
on the other side with a small bunch of village horses, probably
the women's, pastured in a pocket over there to keep them from
drifting away. In addition, Lieutenant De Rudio insisted that
Custer himself appeared on the heights directly across the
stream, waving his hat, apparently in approval. But that point
was far below any crossing to support Reno, as Curly and
Bouyer must have told Custer, and, as nearly as any from Reno's
force could see, very far above other crossings that might be
useful.

After Reno's battalion had advanced in the line for about
a mile, they seemed to be nearing a shallow ravine, or dry
wash, one reaching all the way down from the lowish bluffs on
the left to the river, cutting across the entire bottoms in a sort
of natural breastworks. Occasional puffs of wind lifted the dust
momentarily, exposing the ravine edge here and there, with
lines of Indian heads visible beyond the charging riders, the low
ravine surely full of Sioux. Plainly, this was a time for caution,
with too much eagerness growing among Reno's troops. Both
horses and men were excited by the stink of living dust and gun
powder, by the whoops and war cries, particularly the recruits,
men who did not know about Indian ambushes or that Indian
fighting was to the total death, as surely as the attack against
them was intended.

Major Reno decided to deploy his force as skirmishers between the arm of timber from the river and the rises to his left. Even before this could be done, two horses became unmanageable and bolted ahead, carrying their riders through the Indian line and the shallow ravine into the Hunkpapa, the Sitting Bull village, the uppermost of the great camp, and were torn from their horses there.

Apparently the Indians considered these men the forerunners of a powerful charge, the two troopers bold as warriors might be bold, riding through the enemy to gain honors or death, and to break the fighting courage and will for an overwhelming attack. So the Sioux hurried their own charge in great force, coming on their finest horses, painted, the tails tied up for war, with feathered manes and jaw ropes. Their spearheading attack was not toward the soldiers but against the scouts along the low bluffs on the left flank, forcing back the section held by their old, old enemies, the Rees. These Indians recognized the power of the coming charge, understood the number of warriors along the Little Bighorn that day, and fled, most of them whipping clear back across the river where the eight men under Stabbed were gathering and trying to hold the small bunches of Sioux horses.

Even with his left flank collapsed, Reno realized that the Sioux should be fighting harder than this so near their standing village, and he dared not proceed without strong reinforcement. There was no support anywhere in sight, Benteen probably fifteen miles up the river and Custer—who could guess where Custer was now? Certainly not any man who knew that he did not support Major Elliott and his men on the Washita, had not even tried to rescue their bodies.

With the dubious aid of the Indian scouts gone—all except Bloody Knife, who had been out gathering up three loose Sioux horses, and one or two Rees lost somewhere in the dust and smoke—Varnum and Hare were left with the crumbled flank and a handful of men. Reno ordered G Troop thrown into the gap now that the Sioux were advancing and firing more daringly than ever in the shielding dust, and retreating to lure the troopers into ambush. Reno thought of the trails that led to the river here, trails of at least five thousand fighting men or more, the scouts had said. He had believed them, and now he was faced by at least five–six hundred warriors with little over one hundred men, since the two were carried into the Indian camp and the two couriers were hurried out to Custer.

Plainly, the major's position was desperate, and yet he felt he must try to hold the bottoms a little longer for the promised support to come, and so he flung up his hand, setting his horse back on its haunches. "Halt!" he ordered the troop commanders, "halt and prepare to fight afoot!"

There was some confusion as the men dismounted and the horse-holders, all veterans, grabbed the bridles, four each, and galloped the horses into the timber toward a central clearing. The thin line of foot soldiers wavered at first and shrank from the crack and whine of the bullets about them and the pale zing of arrows, but they steadied and began to fire at the whooping warriors sweeping up and wheeling in the billowing yellow dust and blue powder smoke, the Indians clinging to the far side of their horses. One warrior, stripped, had wrapped a company banner around his body and raced his war horse five times past the line of troopers, drawing bullets like hail about him and getting away untouched.

In response to a rallying, the line of troopers slipped forward 100 yards or so, one man after another, led by veterans crawling, dodging from hollow to weed to sage clump to prairie-dog mound under the shielding smoke. They stopped as a little wind lifted the cover of dust and gunfire for a moment and showed a solid wall of racing and whooping horsemen and beyond them the blackened pole tops of skin lodges thick as a forest. The line halted and began to fire rapidly from knee and belly. Almost at once a sergeant was killed and a couple of other men hit as the Sioux swooped in, shooting point-blank. They got what they wanted: an excited and blinding roar of guns, the ammunition largely wasted in the dust, the firing so fast that the barrels of the carbines heated and the swollen cartridges jammed in the breeches, the cursing men hacking away at the empty casing with their knives so they could fire again, perhaps compelled to go to the pistol.

Reno had moved up and down the line to calm the men— over 15 per cent under their first fire—to slow their need to shoot at any distance. He was near Captain Moylan when word came from the timber that the Sioux were massing on the far side of the river and slipping across to the timber to get at the horses. Leaving Lieutenant Hodgson to keep him informed of the situation on the firing line, Reno risked taking G Troop— the smallest, under thirty-five men—to the brush at the river bank. From there he got a good view of the upper lodges and could see the Indians scattered all along the stream, coming and going in painted, dusty swarms, some guarding the women and children fleeing down the river, fresh warriors whipping up, apparently from camps lower down.

But there was no way to stop the Indians still creeping in through the underbrush and dust past G Troop to infiltrate the horse-holders, pricking a couple of the best animals with arrows, making them break away, to be swept off by yelling youths. It was a desperate moment, for in ten minutes the troops could all be set afoot and run down like rabbits fleeing through the grass. Major Reno hurried out upon the open bottoms, trying to get beyond the dust, to make a last search of the horizon for his support, any support. There was nothing, only the roar of battle back around the timber, and far bullets spurting around him as Sioux sharpshooters tried to pick him off. He signaled for his adjutant. Hodgson came galloping up, his young face dirt-streaked and disturbed: The Sioux were passing around the left of the firing line with little opposition and gathering behind it.

They couldn't hold out long here, the young lieutenant had to say.

The major nodded, wiping the stinging dust from his eyes and the sweat from his mustache with a bandanna. Once more he looked back to the river crossing, past the hanging dust blued by gunsmoke, and beyond, where Sioux charged out to recapture some horses that the Rees were running off into the breaks. But there was no blue-britched battalion in sight, no support, although it was practically an hour and half since he had struck the Little Bighorn, and his two couriers were either lost or ignored. By now Custer might be five–six miles down the river. Perhaps he had discovered the half-dozen "Sioux lodges," enough lodges whose defeat would make him, as he had promised the Rees, the Great Father. Perhaps he was on the way to a telegraph office himself by now, to Bozeman or the Platte with the news of a victory to stampede the Democratic Convention, either through the rumored inside track he had with James Gordon Bennett's men there, or with those of Gould's *World*. Then there might be friendly delegates from Michigan, in spite of some apparently leaning toward Hendricks. Surely someone in the home delegation was waiting in St. Louis for the news of victory.

Even so, there should be some sign of McDougall and the pack string, at least the ammunition mules belonging to Reno's three troops, with the troop escorts. Perhaps the Sioux had finally decided to capture the strung-out train, as the major had feared every day since they left the Yellowstone, or Mc-

Dougall might have been ordered straight to Custer. Even without orders, he would probably follow Custer's trail, the heavier, plainer one, and leave Reno surrounded by yelling Sioux and his guns empty.

It was a time beyond the bitterest profanity. Only the scattering of veteran sharpshooters among the troopers were holding the Indians off now, and soon their guns would be empty if the battalion wasn't overrun before. Reno and his subordinates knew by now that he would have to proceed as though there wasn't another soldier in the whole country, and clearly he would have to act soon or he would lose at least the depleted troops of the firing line. Temporarily, he could draw them into the thickets around the spreading cottonwoods that sheltered the horses, but there was no telling how many Indians had worked up the arm of the brush to the timber, creeping as quiet as bullsnakes as they did elsewhere, through rushes, weeds, and sagebrush, not even a grasshopper aroused to jump and betray them as they passed.

Out at the firing line, Lieutenant Wallace, who had heard Cooke's orders to Reno after the division of the command, was desperate too. He had remained out when Lieutenant McIntosh withdrew his G Troop to guard the horses. Seeing Captain Moylan through the smoke, Wallace shouted that another courier should be sent to hurry up Custer's promised support.

But who? Not Terry's courier Herendeen, with a good horse but not familiar with every cut and canyon as the courier must be—preferably an Indian who could strip and be a Sioux in the dust. Unfortunately, the few Indians remaining with Reno were strangers to the country, and too much afraid. There was, however, Billy Jackson, breed scout, with friends among the hostiles.

Jackson agreed that the situation was desperate and that a

messenger to Custer was imperative. Then he pointed off toward the river crossing, shut off now by a wild racing of Indian warriors who had turned the left flank, with surely many more hidden along the bank and in the silvery buffalo berry thickets.

"Nobody get through," the scout said, shaking his shaggy head. "Nobody . . ."

The men within hearing looked to each other. He was right.

By now too many troopers were being hit in the thin and scattered firing line, bold warriors charging their horses through it, perhaps to fall and be dragged away by the lariat around the horse's neck, but more coming, always more. Soon the line would be overrun entirely by a determined attack, the Indians clinging to the far side of their mounts by a toe over the back and a hand in the mane while they shot through the flying cloud of hair above the withers or under the neck of the galloping ponies.

Abruptly Major Reno decided to order the men into the timber. They came, stooping, running, faces blackened by dust and powder soot, sweat- and blood-streaked, some going down from bullet or arrow as the warriors whooped them along. A couple of the wounded were gathered up and carried on the run, others helping themselves as well as they could, the dead left behind to be struck with quirt, spear, or bow as the young warriors counted their coups on the bodies, dead or alive.

There was confusion in the timber, too, the officers losing contact with their men in the tangle of thorny rose and plum brush around the scattered cottonwoods and box elders, the whole timber now filled with the roar of panic shooting, and the thickening stink and sting of black powder smoke augmented by fire set along the river by the Indians to eat its slow way toward the brush. Troopers shouted, Indians whooped, whistling bullets ripped the foliage, thudding as they struck wood or flesh, the horses plunging and screaming—his troopers surrounded by four–five times their number, and more warriors constantly arriving from down the river.

Surely Charley Reynolds realized there must be at least five thousand fighting men in the great camp. He knew the southern Oglalas and Brules, the scattering of Minneconjous aligned with them, from his years scouting around the North Platte region. He knew those of the Missouri agencies, too, but less of the hostile Hunkpapas, although he recognized Gall, Crow King, and Knife Chief when they rode in. Gall, usually a peaceful man, had his hair ragged and new mourning striations bleeding for the wife and child he found killed just now when he returned from down near the great central council lodge. Young Black Moon, warrior society leader in the charges against Reno, was killed soon after the troopers were deployed and now Gall and Crow King took over. Reynolds also knew Red Horse, another chief of the great council lodge, and Kills Eagle, from the Blackfoot Sioux up north. He saw the brother of Feather Earrings, a Minneconjou, fall and be dragged away as Red Horn Bull, the famous Oglala runner, led the charge.

Once a great shouting went up for a swarm of warriors from the camps farthest down the river. Reynolds saw them enter the fight, still unbloodied: a great party of Oglalas and Cheyennes led by Crazy Horse, with Hump, head warrior of the Oglalas, riding beside him. He couldn't know that the Oglala war chief had organized the attack on Crook the 17th of June, the first organized Sioux attack in history, strong enough to drive the general from the field. But Reynolds knew Crazy Horse, and knew the attack would take on a new daring, a new wildness, and a new solidarity, with slier attempts at decoying Reno farther on, far enough to surround and overwhelm him.

With the ammunition getting low, Reno drew his defense back from the river bank too now, into a broken circle in the timber. But he knew he must not try to hold out here either—unless he and his men were to remain forever. He could no longer hope for reinforcements. So far as the major or his officers knew, there had been no battle plan, and by now the 7th Cavalry was apparently hopelessly scattered, Benteen and McDougall, perhaps even Custer, in possible difficulties elsewhere, or surely someone would have brought Reno an order, if not support.

Hoping to unite the regiment, as seemed absolutely necessary in the face of the overwhelming enemy, to save his own men from total annihilation, perhaps even the entire regiment of approximately 650, Reno decided to move across the river to the ridge. There he could be seen and he could dispose of his force to hold out until reinforcements, Benteen or McDougall, he hoped, might arrive. And they must come soon, even up there. The men had started with 100 rounds each for the carbines, half in their belts and half in the saddlebags, but the hot exchanges had brought this dangerously low.

The fires in the dead rushes along the river bank had spread both ways into the ripening June grasses of the bottoms and the buffaloberry brush. Now it had reached straight ahead into the higher, drought-withered weeds and burned more rapidly, making a great smoke as it crept along the dusty, dried brush tops in the light northeast wind, blazing up in the tent caterpillar webs, leaving the green wood smoldering, the fire smoke setting even the seasoned, gun-broken cavalry horses wild. Here and there one tore loose, the horse guard leaping into the saddles of the wilder ones, to hold them if possible. On the river side the scorching head of flames drove the troopers back, so the defense was collapsing there, in spite of Reno's frantic efforts to bolster the resistance long enough for an orderly movement. He shouted assurance that no naked Indian would come creeping in from that side, not through the smoldering brush; but his voice was lost in the roar of guns and the snap and pop of the fire.

Sweat-streaked and powder-smoked, the major hurried around the broken circle of his troopers in the timber, trying to be heard, cautioning that the Indians were stealing in under the rolling smoke from downwind, one not over five feet away when a bullet finally drove him into the earth. More horses were struck, screaming as they went down. The men were forced still farther upon themselves. Several more were wounded, one from M Troop so badly that the doctor was found and hurried through the underbrush.

Reno caught a glimpse of interpreter Isaiah Dorman and then of the sooted, resigned face of Charley Reynolds, who had come along on Custer's scout although his gun hand was swollen and infected. Then he had realized the overwhelming number of Sioux sure to be gathered here for their summer conference and angered the colonel by saying this. Girard told Reno he had given Charley a drink of whisky to cheer his gloom, but it didn't help and now there seemed only one purpose left in him. Methodically Charley Reynolds thrust cartridges into the breech of his rifle, and, ignoring the pain in his hand, watched with his customary patience for a warrior charging in close or for the slow, gentle shake of brush that revealed a stealthy Sioux approach. Then he pulled the trigger, ejected the smoking shell to the scattering around him, and threw in another. Bloody Knife, too, had the calm face of the resigned, bending forward, peering through the brush and smoke, his gun ready. The major stopped beside the Ree to ask by sign where the Indians would concentrate their thrust, to help him plan the run for the river and the heights beyond.

Before the scout could answer, a new burst of bullets ripped through the torn foliage. One of them struck Bloody Knife, blowing his skull open and spattering the handsome black

silk kerchief with blue stars that Custer had given to his once-
favorite scout—spatterings that reached Major Reno standing
beside the Ree.

For a moment the hardened campaigner was as sickened as
the rawest recruit. Plainly the Indians were everywhere, pene-
trating everywhere, so many of them that even two–three times
the number of his battalion would not hope to hold out in
this patch of timber. Perhaps not even the entire 7th Cavalry,
with all the ammunition of the pack train, could hold out.
Plainly, he must act fast if he was to save any of his deserted
force, save any at all, even at the sacrifice of leaving the dead
behind.

Waving his pistol, the major shouted his orders to repair to
a new position beyond the river, on the bluffs. In the central
clearing he gave the order to mount and form in columns of
four to Moylan and McIntosh himself and sent Hodgson on
to Captain French, but with the crashing of gunfire, the whooping, the thunder of hoofs, no order by voice could be heard
two yards away. Dust, smoke, and burning brush made communication by signal impossible and Custer had forbidden
trumpets.

Furious at the desertion of his force by the commander, Reno
watched the men come running out of the thickets to the
horses, hoping that all those scattered in the underbrush had
been reached with the order before it was entirely too late, and
that the few wounded could be helped to mount. The dead had
to be left behind, the dead and near-dead, for the withdrawal
could not wait, with the Indians firing into the troopers from
the timber around the clearing. Some men, well hidden, took
the opportunity to avoid the run for the river, Lieutenant De
Rudio of Company A among these, and several soldiers as well
as Herendeen, Girard, Jackson, and other scouts.

Then a trooper was picked off from the middle of Company

M, crying out as he was hit, to slide dead from his horse, the riderless animal loose and crashing through the brush. Now Reno knew they had to move quickly, not wait for the rest. He spurred to the head of Company A to lead the desperate run from the timber and out across the bottoms swarming with Sioux. He realized he would lose many men, but some could be saved this way, the only way, with the predicted overwhelming number of Indians all around him, and the failure of the support promised by Custer, even the failure of the battalion's reserve ammunition. It was a hard choice for a man with four brevets for gallant and meritorious service, now to be hung up like this, where he must watch his men being slaughtered.

Before the charge of the troops toward the river, the Indians parted, catching the column between a cross fire of bullets and arrows from both flanks, particularly from the right, shutting Reno away from the good crossing, forcing him down the river to a narrow one-pony-wide ford cut through the high earth bank down into the soft quicksand of the channel with the same narrow, steep climb out on the far side. Indians afoot were dodging from tree to tree over there and from cut bank to bush, getting into position; while on the mile and a half bottoms that Reno had to cross six–seven hundred mounted Sioux whooped and shot. The troopers replied with their pistols as they spurred ahead, but the expert warriors were sliding to the far side of their galloping ponies, deliberately emptying the army saddles, while others, mostly youths, gathered up the loose cavalry horses. Then, as the hand guns were silenced, the warriors closed in, swinging war clubs, wrestling men from their wild and rearing mounts. Reno emptied one pistol into the Indians and then the other as he tried to hold them off, and to pay them for the men he was losing—particularly the proud Lieutenant McIntosh, of Indian blood too, who went down at the edge of the timber. For this one man alone Reno's fury would have been great—the good soldier sacrificed on this foolish venture today when tomorrow they would have had an army, an army with whom the Sioux could have been "popped like a louse is popped between the thumbnails."

But instead the Indians were free to push in upon his little force, half lost in the new cloud of dust and stinging powder smoke, lost and trapped like a herd of buffaloes, the warriors crowding in, cutting the men down like so many fat yearlings.

At the ford Reno shouted commands to cross single file, but no one could hear him now—not those in front, ridden down by the frantic horse behind, not those behind, driven on by arrow and lead. The stampeding horses plunged forward into the narrow pony crossing, two, three, and more wedging themselves, the water ahead full of men fighting for the yard-wide outlet up the high bank on the far side, indeed like buffaloes caught in a narrow water gorge. Some daring young warriors leaped into the churning stream with knife and war club. After the first troopers lucky enough to get out, the bank sides became slippery from the wet horses and began to break down under the desperate pawing of the ironed hoofs. Men and animals died there under the hot Sioux fire. Lieutenant Hodgson, Reno's adjutant and a favorite of the regiment, tried to avoid the pile-up and leaped his horse off the high bank, but it was struck by a bullet and fell dead in a mighty splash of water, the lieutenant hit in the knee. Grabbing the stirrup of Sergeant Culbertson, he was towed across, only to be shot down after they got out on the far side. Dr. De Wolf managed to reach the far bank too, and then was killed from the bluff above. Davern of Company F, lost his horse to a bullet, but he had kept one cartridge in his pistol. With this he shot the Indian from his pony, leaped upon the bare back, and spurred after the van of troops heading up the old buffalo trail into a draw that narrowed to the ridge, the horses taking the steep rocky climb by heaves and jumps. The troopers who made it felt their lives had been returned to them by sheer luck. Sergeant Ryan of Company M looked back upon the hazed and swarming bottoms and was certain that in a few minutes more down there and not a man would have lived to escape. On the bluff the weary Lieutenant Varnum, hat gone, looking tall as a tree, was holding up his hands to stop the troopers appearing over the steep edge.

"For God's sake, men," he shouted, "don't run. There are officers and men killed and wounded down there and we must go back to get them."

Perhaps some heard him, but plainly it was not voice or command that held most of the men—particularly the green ones, those new to the Indian wars. Only the failure of their horses kept them from fleeing as most of the Indian scouts had fled.

On the broken, unfamiliar ridge Reno tried to find a high spot visible to any scout or courier from far off, and yet offering the best defensive position. He selected a knob topped by a sort of shallow depression to hold the horses and protect the wounded that Dr. Porter was gathering to a shot-torn banner drooping in the hot air. Ten of these had been able to get to the hill mounted. Most of them were from A Troop, which had led the column. Reno turned the care of the wounded over to Captain Moylan, to make them as comfortable and secure as possible. Then, with still no sign of the pack train anywhere, the major sent a man to find McDougall and bring the ammunition mules in on a gallop.

By now some noticed that Reno had also lost his hat in the run for the hill and tied a red bandanna around his head. His mustache and beard were thick with the pale yellow-gray dust caught and crusted in the sweat. Hurrying around on the hill, the major deployed his men, as well as he could at the low depression, to dig into the gravelly, hard-baked earth with all they had—knives and tin cups. The major's dirty face was still streaking with tears over the loss of his adjutant, Hodgson, and over McIntosh and the rest as he tried to take stock.

Three officers were dead, including Dr. De Wolf, and twenty-nine enlisted men and scouts; seven had serious wounds, and fourteen soldiers and scouts were missing, some probably behind in the brush and thickets of the bottoms. Reno and the rest had a fair idea where Lieutenant De Rudio would be, and Herendeen and Girard, too, the latter particularly noted for taking care of his own skin. He and most of the other scouts didn't consider themselves hired to fight; really none except Charley Reynolds, who was either completely disabled or dead, or he would be here. The Rees, probably all except the dead Bloody Knife, had vanished over the ridge toward the mouth of the Powder River—and justifiably so, many thought. They had tried to tell Custer just what would be found here on the Little Bighorn—the great summer conference of the Tetons. Probably twelve to fifteen thousand Indians, they had said, with perhaps twenty thousand horses and at least five to seven thousand fighting men.

As Reno worked out a place of defense, some of the Crow scouts began to slip in out of the canyons. The major welcomed them, hoping to make the best of what remained in men and scanty ammunition—less than five rounds per man, Varnum said. He hoped, too, that the scouts might help hold the Indians off the bodies of Hodgson and De Wolf and the troopers killed on the steep climb to the hill.

It was not too soon, for the Sioux, doubly angered at the killing of High Eagle, a chief of the great council lodge, were beginning to drop bullets in upon them from some of the surrounding ridges. Next it might be prairie fire; although there was very little grass, it was dry. Besides, the hordes of Indians could drag up dead rushes and timber from the river bottoms, push the burning stuff in upon Reno as soon as the wind rose a little, to panic the horses and the green recruits, blind everyone in the smoke, and cut them down.

But one had to hope for the men here on the ridge. Somewhere there were three more sections of the great 7th Cavalry— nine troops more and the pack train with the ammunition so desperately needed. Of these Custer and his five companies had surely passed them by—as the fresh trail of shod horses off on the right beyond Reno's hill showed very clearly—although Moylan tried to believe that the colonel was still in the rear and would come to their assistance.

With a moment to consider their position, the major and his officers spoke about the rumors that firing had been heard far down the river somewhere while the battalion was piled up in the pony crossing of the river. They listened now, with hands cupped to ears, but there was no sound other than the Indians shooting and yelling around them, nothing else except the faint whooping from the village below, still largely hidden by the rise of brush- and grass-fire smoke on the bottoms, although the dust down there was drifting away over the prairie. Women were all over the fighting ground, their knives glinting occasionally in the pale sunlight—women hurrying here and there, like small running specks, hacking and then running again.

The Indians around Reno seemed in no great hurry, perhaps depending upon time: lack of ammunition and thirst could do the job without the loss of another warrior.

4 RENO ON THE HILL

★ ★ ★ ★ ★ ★ ★ ★

The consultation of Custer with his adjutant, their weary horses standing quietly together while the men worked over the notebook, had produced a battalion of three companies for Benteen, and his orders to strike off on a valley hunt, as he called it. The captains of the added troops were Godfrey and Weir, both fellow Ohioans of the Custers. Weir was a particular partisan of the commander from his four years, to a lieutenant colonelcy, in the 3rd Michigan Cavalry—the unit that had mutinied against Custer in 1865—and had testified for the colonel in the court-martial of 1867.

Weir and Godfrey looked back to their colonel as the new battalion was being set up. Then they fell in behind Benteen as he led out, trot and walk, from one line of high bluffs to the next, seeking an unknown valley harboring Indians and holding himself ready to "pitch into" any he could find. The terrain along the breaks of the Rosebud and the Wolf Mountains was unfailingly rough and rocky, largely bare of grass, sage, or weeds, with no sign of hoofprint anywhere, pony or buffalo, or even a prairie sparrow to rise before the marching column. No one with the battalion had ever been anywhere near the region, and although the six Crow scouts of the regiment knew every knob and canyon of the country, as did Jackson, Bouyer, and even Reynolds, none of these was sent with Benteen.

But the captain with the thick thatch of gray curls darkened by the fine dust of the day's march was an experienced Plains campaigner and experienced, too, in the ways of his commander. It was not the first curious detail assigned to him, but perhaps the most curious, with trails of a great camp ahead of the regiment—trails of far too many Indians for the whole 7th to face, if the scouts were right. In the meantime Benteen had been sent off to the left into the lifeless wilds, with a fourth of the force.

As the battalion drew farther and farther from the command, the captain knew he had to come to some decision. There was no Indian sign anywhere and no sign or smell of water for the thirsty men and horses, while the trail Custer was following had offered plenty of both. Judging by the lag in both the Weir and Godfrey companies, nobody wanted to be left out of the coming fight somewhere behind them. Besides, the help of his three troops, with the lowest per cent of recruits never exposed to gunfire, might be welcome, even crucial.

Benteen had considered his orders militarily senseless from the start, whatever Custer's personal reasons for sending him far from any possible action by the regiment. Now he decided to ignore the instructions to hunt that unknown valley. He recalled his advance guard and struck diagonally across to the probable direction of Ash Creek and Custer's march, hoping by speed on the easier downslope of the general terrain to make up for the precious time lost in the futile valley hunt. Riding well ahead of his force, Benteen reached the trail with the scant droppings of Custer's horses still drying, but with no mule tracks except those of Mark Kellog's animal and of the one assigned to the Ree, Stabbed, when his pony gave out. At the boggy place Benteen spent perhaps fifteen minutes trying to water his thirsting animals a little. Just as the battalion lined out again, the advance mules of the supply train thundered up at an awkward gallop, packs pounding and flapping, the guards trying with yell and spur to head the animals, but unable to keep the leaders from plunging straight into the bogs, some going down to their packs in the mud.

Benteen looked back but he couldn't spare the time to help in the extrication, which was the responsibility of the train escort, large enough for all such contingencies if not for a stand against the Sioux. He followed the fresh trail along the left of Ash Creek. A mile or so below the lone tipi, still smoldering, Sergeant Kanipe came riding in from Custer with Cooke's written orders to the commander of the mule train to hurry the packs. Benteen sent the man on to McDougall, some miles back by now. As Kanipe passed the column he shouted, "We got 'em, boys!" seeming to imply that Custer had attacked the village and captured it. But the message increased Benteen's uneasiness about serious trouble, and with his orderly he hurried on, riding four–five hundred yards ahead of his battalion to draw them along, the eager Captain Weir about midway between him and the column.

Before long, Benteen saw another man come whipping up the trail. It was Trumpeter Martin, his lathered and worn horse staggering along as fast as it could go. The man handed over a scrawled and abbreviated message from Cooke: "*Benteen Come on Big Village Be quick Bring packs W. W. Cooke*" and a postscript, difficult to read: "*Brng Pacs.*"

Benteen looked down the trail in alarm, but all he could see was a riderless horse, perhaps played out and left behind.

"What is happening?" he demanded.

The Indians were skedaddling, abandoning the village, Martin told the captain in his broken Italian-English—natural from the immigrant Martini enlisted under the Anglicized name of Martin. It had taken the trumpeter three-quarters of an hour to get from Custer to Benteen, and about fifteen minutes since he looked down into the river valley and saw the fighting there. But Benteen, not knowing of Custer's later division of his force, did not ask about Reno, and Martin volunteered nothing of the fight. He said that probably Custer had made a charge through the Indian village by this time.

This limited information seemed to reduce the urgency. There was no sound of firing, so instead of hurrying back to the pack train himself, Benteen gave Martin a note to McDougall. By then the trumpeter had been issued another horse. His was not only played out, but it had picked up a bullet in the hip somewhere along the route.

"You're lucky it wasn't you!" Benteen told the courier.

But the bullet was tangible evidence to underline the need for the packs. The captain waited until Weir came up and showed him Cooke's message, asking no questions and receiving no volunteered advice. By this time Benteen felt he had some sense of the situtation. If he went back for the packs, which could be moved only so fast after the long marches, valuable time would be lost getting his battalion to Custer, who at least needed his ammunition. If he halted to wait for the packs, there was no gain except protection for the train from Indian attack, unlikely now. So he took the trot along the fresh trail of what seemed part of Custer's force and gradually raised the vibration of far gunfire. The sound of shooting grew distinct as Benteen neared the Little Bighorn along the lodgepole trail that was surely headed for a crossing. Once his horse pricked up its ears and looked off toward the breaks to the right, but it was only the breed Curly, one of Custer's scouts, slipping away as most of the Rees had done.

The sound of battle grew louder and more continuous, more pronounced and insistent. The captain ordered a gallop with drawn pistols, expecting to see the enemy around every bend, the Sioux being driven toward him by Custer.

Benteen was forming a line to meet the fleeing enemy when he came into full view of the Little Bighorn and stopped his troopers. The river valley was full of dust and smoke from the powder, and from the grass that the Indians had fired. The field glasses showed a scattered engagement about two miles down, with gunshots and moving specks visible through the glass, fleeing specks, friend or foe, strung across the river and up the steep bluff on this side. With the high ridge rising there and pushing close to the stream for some miles—bluffs difficult to climb under fire if he were driven out too—Benteen hesitated to charge over into the milling Sioux.

Several Indians appeared back behind the bluffs to the right of the river, stopped their horses to look, and then whipped up with a small herd of captive ponies. They were Crow scouts; one of them shouted, "Many Sioux!" to Benteen and made the signs of "big fight." Another pointed back along the top of the river ridge where some soldiers were coming together, bent low on their horses, kicking them to keep them going. More appeared over the steep rim of the bluff, some stumbling up afoot, perhaps dragging at their blown horses. Here and there a trooper looked back and fired against some enemy hidden in the breaks below, the puff of smoke a blue explosion, and then moved to a point where a man—not Custer, but Reno—was gesturing toward a planted banner, gesturing direction and haste.

Benteen lowered his glasses and deployed his force into a skirmish line along the river side of the steep bluffs, hoping to hold back the Indians swarming up from the bottoms. When Reno's troops gathering on the hill saw Benteen's battalion, loud cheers went up from them—cheers intended for Custer's five companies, come to the rescue at last. The pursuing Indians stopped at sight of the new troops, whoever they were—four or five hundred Indians on the highest point of land about a mile away, surprised in the attack on the little knot of troopers, with about nine hundred more warriors still milling around on the bottoms and stringing over the river.

Major Reno came riding down to meet Captain Benteen. He was still hatless, with the red bandanna around his head against the heat and the vagrant sun, his face, his mustache and bearding caked with dust. He was excited, and furious at what he called the betrayal of his men by the commander's failure to support them. He greeted Benteen most gratefully; his arrival was a damned welcome surprise. When he last saw the captain he seemed headed off beyond the Rosebud Mountains on some long, long route.

"Where is Custer?" Benteen asked, unaware even now that the command had been divided once more after his departure. To Reno's explosive, "I don't know!" the captain produced Cooke's message to bring the packs. It seemed Custer had forgotten about the order to go valley-hunting, and if Benteen hadn't finally decided to ignore, to disobey, the command, he could have been twenty, even twenty-five miles from the packs and the trail when Martin came to find him, pushing his horse, already failing, as far as it could go.

But Reno and his men knew even less about Custer's whereabouts than the order for the packs suggested. From French, Moylan, Varnum, and Wallace, stopping by at intervals to welcome Benteen, there was anger and curses, for their colonel—running off and leaving them hanging after he ordered them to attack the village. It wasn't that he didn't know exactly

where they were, not after he sent Cooke and Keogh along
as far as the river crossing, where the rising dust of the Sioux
warriors was plain to see. And when the Indians, far too strong,
pressed hard, the major had sent two couriers back, at intervals,
for the promised support. Nothing had been heard of them or
of any reinforcements. Reno had seen nothing of Custer since
several miles back, although some of the men said they caught
a glimpse of him on a bluff down the river, from their position
on the hill here, and some told him now that they heard firing
from down farther. Reno assumed that was Custer, as Cooke's
message to Benteen and Martin's words seemed to corroborate.
But there was no sign of the pack train and Reno's ammunition
was dangerously low, even for a stand up here, where he could
be seen, be reached by McDougall.

On Benteen's asurance that the mule train could not be very
far away by now, Reno asked Lieutenant Hare, acting as his
adjutant in Hodgson's place, to go hurry the packs along as
much as possible. But young Hare's horse was spent. Offered a
choice of Benteen's force, the freshest remaining because he
might have to outrun a lot of Sioux, the lieutenant slipped down
to shake hands with Captain Godfrey, his commander in K
Troop, and to accept his horse for the attempt.

"We had a big fight in the bottoms and got whipped," Hare
called back as he spurred away.

Captain Benteen divided his practically untouched ammunition supply with Reno's men, particularly with the 15 per cent
of itchy-trigger-fingered recruits. Yet Lieutenant Varnum, wild
with sorrow when he discovered that his friend Hodgson was
dead, had blazed away at Indians hopelessly out of reach even
with a borrowed rifle for its range over the carbine. Reno had
fired the same hopeless shots because so many men had been
lost, particularly his brave young adjutant, lost by the mis-
calculations of his superiors. All that could be done for Lieu-

tenant Hodgson now was to try to keep the Indians from where his body probably lay.

Benteen, grim at what he saw on the ridge, with so many Indians swarming to the attack, hurried to help form the defense. No one could tell how powerful or protracted the attack might be, with the semicircle of higher ridges blocking out most of both the village and the Little Bighorn farther down. He looked around the men, the shaken survivors, and realized that even with his three fresh companies, all of Reno Hill could be overrun here in the next twenty minutes, perhaps with guns from the pack train, which would have to break through the tightening circle of attack.

Facing this nightmare that had confronted Reno one way or another since he led his troops in a gallop across the bottoms, it was decided to keep most of Benteen's fresh force along the bluff face below the major's position. There the troops could see two–three miles of the bottoms with part of the river ridge and surely detect any large body of Indians creeping up from the stream. But those coming up behind the heights, from above and below, could not be detected until they caught the little circle on Reno Hill in their cross fire. Besides, there must be reinforcements ready, stout and resolute men, to go help the pack train through the gathering siege. The gunfire was already breaking into bursts of drumming roar around the hill, some of the bullets whining as they struck the loose rock and pebbles, to ricochet dangerously. But here, too, the bow was a telling weapon in the hands of the few expert warriors who managed to creep near and drop arrows among the horses and the wounded without lifting a dusty head to sight.

For a necessary moment several officers collected in a pocket at the edge of the bluff, to plan as they peered over into the valley full of thinning haze, with fresh dust and smoke creeping across the snake bends of the river farther down, surely from some other engagement. There were still many Indians down the river, some collected in standing knots along the bottoms, some whipping back and forth or stopping in rows to look up toward the heights downstream, some of them so far away they seemed bits of burned grass blowing along, lodging here and there and drifting again toward the river and out of sight.

Up on the heights the Indians were sharpening their attack on Reno, pushing in from every side, even along the bluff face. More young warriors with their paint caked in yellow-gray dust moved like bullsnakes toward their prey, creeping slowly, imperceptibly, from hollow to little cut bank, to weed clump, driving a silent arrow into any careless movement. More, too, farther out, were lifting their bows upward and letting the sharp iron points fall into the little circle of men and horses.

Yet the overwhelming charge expected any moment did not come, giving the diggers who tried to throw up small breastworks from the hard-baked and rocky soil a little time while the sharpshooters watched to hold the Indians back. The officers kept returning to the one question that had no answer. Some asked it laudatorily, as Captain Weir, who had lost no men, had no blood and brains splattered over him; some who had charged unsupported into the waiting horde of Indians on the bottoms profanely: Where was Custer?

Captain Moylan, a veteran in Plains warfare, was heavy with the weight of the injured upon him, many too wounded to flee as the Indian scouts had done, even if there were enough strong horses left to carry them beyond the Sioux. He offered one remark: "Gentlemen, in my opinion, General Custer has made the biggest mistake of his life not taking the whole regiment at once into the first attack."

There were dark looks from the Custer partisans, but Varnum the white linen hankerchief still around his head, recalled now that when he was trying to hold the Indians off the dead and wounded down toward the river he had heard some far-off firing—just a hard burst, not a volley, but a short hot exchange lasting a few minutes. Lieutenant Wallace was beside him at the time, and he had said, "Jesus Christ, Wallace, hear that—and that!"

It seemed some miles off and Varnum said he thought that Custer was having a warm time of it, but before long the shooting was done.

Others repeated now that they had seen Custer and Cooke on the ridge while Reno was fighting down on the bottoms, with some disagreement about the actual time and the exact point and whether his field glasses reflected a momentary bit of sun through the thin clouds. Still, even without the glasses, he could see the skirmish line by the puffs of smoke and all the Indians massed at the front and understand how badly the fight was going. Bare-eyed, he surely saw that the valley was full of smoke and dust and alive with thousands of Indians like fierce ants disturbed at a new nest.

Benteen considered these stories carefully and decided that Custer's appearance on the ridge was about the time Trumpeter Martin was sent back with the message to bring the packs. The repetition of the scrawl "Brng pacs" seemed to indicate that at least the writer, Cooke, was excited or wanted to assure special protection for the mule train. From the point where Custer had stood, miles of river valley were visible, with large camp circles and thousands of riding Indians. Now he must have realized something of the desperate situation his scouts had predicted ever since they saw the first of the gathering trails. But perhaps not. He had, after all, told luncheon guests in New York that his regiment could whip all the Indians on the Plains . . .

Possibly Captain Weir, too, began to understand something of the power of the Sioux here; more probably he was anxious

to be in the fight beside his old commander in the 3rd Michigan
Cavalry for the glory of it. There were some words with Reno,
impatient words, Weir insisting that the force push down to
where Custer must be. But there was not enough ammunition
for a protracted stand, not enough to risk leaving such protection as they had here before the mule train arrived, let alone
to break through the Indian encirclement. Surely Custer expected to be short himself, judging by the anxious messages
he sent out for the packs. Besides, Reno's troops had gone
through a terrible battle, his men and horses both exhausted,
and with many stretcher-wounded who must be carried afoot.

Angrily, Weir went to find his lieutenant, Edgerly, while in
the little depression behind him Dr. Porter and his aides were
working with the wounded, to stop the bleeding, ease the pain,
and protect them as much as possible from the firing from a
height off northward, more bullets and arrows dropping among
the horses too. In the meantime the troopers were getting the
range and spying out gullies and little ravines where the Indian
bowmen were hiding. There had been no movement down
where Sergeant Culbertson said Hodgson's body probably lay.
The firing of Reno and then Varnum seemed to have kept the
Indians off until Benteen arrived. Now, with the capable captain to take command, even if his major should not return,
Reno decided on a little foray to save at least the body of his
loyal adjutant and to get some of the canteens refilled for the
wounded, fevering in the swelter of windless heat, Moylan
begging for water for them. Armed with carbine and pistols,
he gathered a small party of volunteers—ten or twelve draped
with strings of empty canteens—and with Culbertson, at whose
stirrup Hodgson had crossed the river, the major started down
the ravine, running low, dodging to bank and washout. The
guns of the Indians hidden along the bluffs broke into an
echoing of explosions, the steep slopes suddenly bursting with

puffs of blue smoke, the Indians slipping from behind puffs before the troopers could reply, earth and broken sand rock spurting up around Reno's little party strung out along the draw. For a while a couple of the Indians hid their location by shooting through rawhide sacks slipped over the guns and extending well past the muzzles to catch the smoke as it erupted. They wounded two troopers, but were no more dangerous than several bow warriors who got up close, the arrow betraying neither its man nor its direction by sight or sound.

The water detail had to cross an open stretch of bottoms, running low, one man hit, the others dropping flat at the edge of the stream. They crept around a dead trooper sprawled down the bank and, with bullets throwing up mud and water over them, tried to fill the canteens that an Indian sharpshooter with a bitter sense of humor punctured or knocked from the hand. Too many men were struck, and reluctantly the party was ordered to retreat to cover, the bullets from the carbines above attempting to hold the Indians back, out of range.

Culbertson had located Hodgson, his sweat-streaked, sooted young face turned toward the sky and already grayed in death. The lieutenant's watch and chain were gone but not the West Point class ring, and in the midst of bullets and flying gravel, Major Reno stooped to work the ring from the dead man's finger. He searched the pockets and located some keys, his men shouting warnings to him of Indians creeping close and the bullets striking all around him. Reno buttoned the findings in his pocket, then, with his broad mouth clamped tight in the dirty stubble of bearding, he ran through the bullets that tore up the ravine as it had been torn during their earlier struggle for the top. Once he looked back, but he could not ask any man to help carry Hodgson's body up through this, could not make himself risk more men.

Further on, a G Troop man came creeping out of a brushy

wash not far from where he had lost his horse on the climb
from the river. But perhaps he should have remained hidden,
for in spite of the desperate measures of Benteen's men to keep
the Indians back, it seemed neither he nor Reno or the rest
could live to reach the hill. Then the attack seemed to slacken
a little as they neared the top, or perhaps it was the fire from
the Weir and Edgerly troops, who had moved around to the
northward, that helped drive those Indians back. What seemed
more probable was that the Indians were running out of ammunition, scarce ever since the sale to them was prohibited long
ago. Reno, on the upper Plains most of the last three–four
years, was aware of the desperate attempts the Sioux made to
get the outlawed arms and powder from traders, from the Red
River breeds of Canada, and even from a medicine man who
claimed he could build guns and ammunition by magic.

When Reno got back to his command, Lieutenant Hare was
coming in with two pack mules loaded with ammunition, a
couple of men for each animal, one ahead jerking the mule
along in a slow, awkward lope that was maintained by a trooper
riding behind, whipping the narrow dusty rump, whipping and
cursing. One of the troopers was crying in his fury at the stub-
bornness of the breed, though the mule was worn out, as many
of the horses were, as his own mount was, the animal's sides
bloody from the roweling of the spurs to keep up the staggering
run. Lieutenant Hare was embarrassed by the hoarse cheers his
arrival brought, saying that they had less trouble getting through
to the command than seemed possible when he left. Where
were most of the Indians from back of the ridge going—heading
northward?

It was true that the firing was slacking off on the other sides
too. The warriors remaining to guard Reno were going to picket
their horses out of reach of gunfire down where there was grass.
But many rode away, and as the lull increased, the men on Reno

Hill listened for far gunshots, but there had been none that anyone could hear for certain since that violent burst mentioned by Varnum and some of those along the ridge a while ago.

It was just as well that the Indian attack had cooled, for now a few men from each side left their positions and ran openly to the two pack mules for ammunition for their fellows. Some pried at the lids of the heavy wooden boxes, but one corporal had a hatchet at his belt and with this he chopped a box to pieces and doled the cartridges out by the double handfuls.

While Major Reno was out with the water detail, Weir, who had never fought the Sioux, started off along the ridge downstream, riding alone. Lieutenant Edgerly, thinking the captain had Reno's permission to go, followed with D Troop from Benteen's battalion. When the major saw Weir and the company off on a knob to the north, he sent Hare to him with orders to communicate with Custer if possible. As soon as the pack train was safely reunited with the troops and the wounded cared for from the pack pharmacy, he would leave the hill and follow.

As soon as the pressure decreased, Edgerly started on again, down a ravine and along the ridge that ran parallel between the river and Custer's trail, plain now, off to the right, along the far slope. But from his higher point Weir could see a large force of Indians head for the lieutenant to cut him off from behind. He signaled the danger and orders to change direction. Edgerly moved over to the high point near Weir's men and remained there, not seriously molested. They could see Indians riding back and forth a couple of miles farther on, and shooting at something or at least shooting now and then.

Finally, around five o'clock or a little later by most of the watches of the outfit, McDougall came up with the pack train. Reno talked to French about burying Hodgson and some others along the bluff and the river while the ammunition and extra campaign hats were being distributed and the wounds treated. With two spades from the packs Varnum started down to help. By this time the Indians along the river and the bluff face seemed practically gone, so that thirteen men and Herendeen, the courier who was to have been sent to Terry from Tullock's Creek, came out of hiding down in the timber. They were fired on by five Indians still watching the river, but managed to drive them off and hurried up to rejoin the command. They all had good explanations: they had lost their horses in the stampede for the river, and hid, largely because there were several wounded men among them.

By the time Reno's arms and ammunition were back to battle standard there was another volley, far off downriver, either combat or a unison firing to celebrate a victory. The major recalled the burial detail and led his command out in a column of twos, heading down toward Custer's supposed position, hoping for a reunion of the entire regiment before the Indians returned to the attack, as they surely would. Hare, with his orders to Weir to open communication with Custer delivered, returned and met the command coming down the river, even Moylan, encumbered by the wounded carried in horse blankets by six men each and moving very slowly. The pack train was coming too, although still farther behind.

Gradually the weary and worn troopers lined out, sharpshooters keeping off any snipers who might remain, the two battalions moving along the heights, clearly visible from far off. On the highest bluff about a mile out Reno and his men stopped, looking past Weir's point to the twisted ridges and ravines down the river. They could hear nothing, but the air ahead was full of dust and smoke, with a spreading cloud above it like a transparent disintegrating thunderhead. About two miles off, knots of horsemen stood together here and there, some moving enough so they could be identified as Indians, but no one understood what they were doing.

Suddenly someone noticed a curious expanse off left of the river. The gradual slopes of grassy prairie looked as though fire had scorched the foliage of a vast stretch of brush, moving brush. Finally some of the men realized what it was: an immense pony herd such as none here had ever seen, heading perhaps to water or to new pasture. The one herd must have been a large part of the twenty thousand head that the Rees had predicted would be brought together here in the annual summer council of the Teton Sioux.

Twenty thousand head of horses they had said and perhaps eight–ten thousand warriors, counting all from thirteen to eighty years of age, and all the usual visitors.

By now some of that warrior force had seen the troops watching on the ridge, and several thousand, it seemed, began to swarm toward them in long strings coming up the slopes. Reno was certain neither Weir's position nor his could be defended, the first wave of warriors threatening to roll Weir back upon the rest, perhaps roll them all together like an Indian woman rolling up a lodge skin. Even Weir saw the impracticality of going farther, and Lieutenant Hare, realizing the danger, used Major Reno's name to order the advance units to return. When the heavy firing began, Weir hurried his withdrawal, leaving an injured man behind crying, pleading not to be left for Indian revenge. Godfrey's company acted as rear guard, taking the heavy fire of the Sioux attack as Weir and the others retreated, some passing Moylan and his wounded in their hurry to regain the scant protection of Reno Hill.

»▶ »▶ »▶ »▶ »▶ »▶ »▶ »▶

5 THE MAN
AGAINST
THE SKY

★ ★ ★ ★ ★ ★ ★ ★

The morning of June 25 the scouts had drawn a map of the Ash Creek region with a weed stalk in the dust for Custer, showing the terrain all the way from the saddle between Davis Creek and the upper dry wash of Ash to the bluffs pushing up against the Little Bighorn. Carefully they marked the ancient lodgepole trail down the creek to the river, indicating where the first live water would be found.

When Custer's chestnut-sorrel, Vic, saddle-sore and weary too, began to faunch at the smell of water ahead, the colonel signaled for a stop to let the stock drink a little, turning back in the saddle to glance over his troopers, men picked for his purpose this crucial day and its afternoon. Benteen was far off in the breaks somewhere, ordered left at an angle to the line of march, to seek out one valley and then the next and the next, although there had been no sign of trail or track that way. Reno was some distance ahead of the colonel, following along the far left side of the little valley of Ash Creek, with orders to make all prudent haste to the river and to charge the Indian village beyond, with the promise of full support.

The colonel let his horse drink too, but pulled the animal back, warning his commanders against too much water, the thirst-frantic stock of the five troops given turns at the little pools, to nuzzle the greening scum away and drink to the muddy bottoms, or to suck up the thin thread of flow in the summer creek. For about five minutes the commander rested, then he was back in the saddle, his face gaunt and wind-burned, his eyes bloodshot from dust and loss of sleep. But he started briskly, followed close by his color bearers and his orderly, not down the creek with the spreading trail of cavalry dust along the far side. Instead he turned right, behind a low ridge that shut him and his men from the sight of Reno, and up a shallow ravine to the rougher, barer heights back from the river.

With Custer rode the dash and color of the 7th Cavalry, the men who had given the regiment the aura of far adventure so envied by the millions caught in lives of hopeless mundanity. Besides the colonel only three were Military Academy men— Lieutenants Porter and Harrington (the latter one of Custer's favored Michiganders), and Second Lieutenant Sturgis, son of the regimental colonel, of last year's class—three Point men in the whole five troops. Benteen, the ranker sent off up the river, had two in his three troops and Reno, sent over to attack the Sioux camp, had five in his three, including the major himself. Custer had the soldiers of fortune: the swaggering Irishman, Miles Keogh, apparently from the French Foreign Legion and the Papal Guard; Cooke of the "Queen's Own" of Canada; and the cripple-armed Smith of the Gray Horse Troop. Young Captain George Yates, Custer's favorite from his home town of Monroe, Michigan, was the brother of Frank Yates, trader at Red Cloud Agency, down in Nebraska, the trader who was still charged with graft in moving the Spotted Tail Agency four years ago. Back in February, young Captain Yates had ordered ammunition directly from the Chief of Ordnance, War Department, Washington. In April he wrote again, demanding the requested ammunition immediately for Custer's expedition going out May 1. He was informed that the order had not been received and that his lettter was being referred to the Department of Dakota, with a chilly reminder that there was a commanding officer, Major Marcus Reno, right at Fort Lincoln, and the usual chief of ordnance in the Department itself. Mark Kellogg, along against Sherman's explicit orders, carried a romantic aura as a writing man, a correspondent. Even Trumpeter Martin, detailed from Benteen's H Troop as orderly to Custer, was said to have been drummer boy for Garibaldi. Then there was the Custer family: the dashing Lieutenant Colonel George Armstrong himself; the roistering Captain Tom; the sickly young civilian Boston; Autie Reed, the favored nephew; and Lieutenant Calhoun, the pampered brother-in-law.

Once away from Ash Creek and the other battalions, Custer led out at his usual gallop, up along the far slope of the ridges that Mitch Bouyer and the Crow scouts told him lay like the backbones of a bunch of ancient mares between them and the Little Bighorn, a mile and a half or two away. Custer had sent White Swan and Half Yellow Face off to the river ridge to see what the Sioux were doing. They went, but joined Reno's scouts and did not return. Later the colonel dispatched the four Crows left to him, including the youth Curly, with similar orders. In the meantime the command moved slowly, but hurried on again after the scouts returned with confirmation of lodges stretched for a long way down the river valley, the upper end full of mounted Indians charging back and forth, shooting at Reno's column moving over the bottoms toward them.

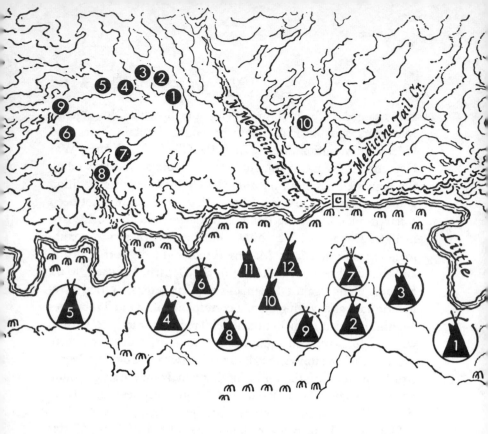

BATTLE OF THE LITTLE BIGHORN

June 25-26, 1876

(Map Based on U.S. Geological Survey, 1891, and Military and Indian Accounts)

HIGH POINTS: A—Custer lookouts over Reno fight. B—Reno Hill. C—Weir Point. D—Probably farthest Reno advance. E—Indians commanding later attacks on Reno.

CUSTER BODIES: 1—Calhoun's command. 2—Lt. Jas. Calhoun. 3—J. J. Crittenden. 4—Capt. M. W. Keogh. 5—Keogh's command. 6—Commands of Capts. Yates and Custer. 7—Dr. G. E. Lord. 8—Lt. Smith's command. 9—Custer Hill: Col. G. A. Custer; Lts. W. W. Cooke, A. E. Smith, W. V. W. Reily; Capt. T. W. Custer nearby. 10—Sgt. Butler.

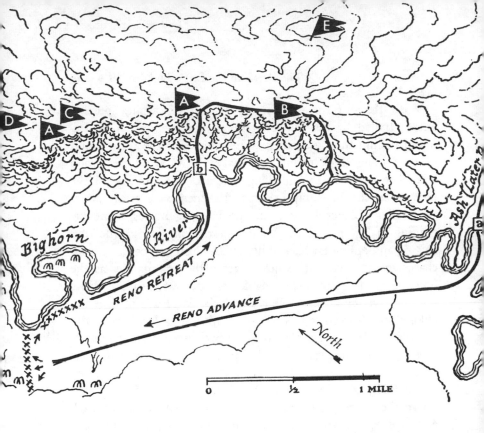

 CROSSINGS: (a) Ancient lodge trail and buffalo ford. (b) Steep, narrow pony ford. (c) Marshy pony ford.

 INDIAN CAMPS: (*In village circles here, due to lack of ground space, instead of usual great circle at Bear Butte, S.D.*)
1—Hunkpapa. 2—Minneconjous. 3—No Bows. 4—Oglalas.
5—Northern Cheyennes, guest tribe. 6—Brules.
7—Blackfoot Sioux. 8—Yanktons. 9—Santees.

LODGES:
10 and 11—Warrior societies guarding council lodge.
12—Great lodge of annual council, poles 18 feet long.

WICKIUPS and shelters for young warriors

With this information Custer started off again, spurring ahead, trailed by his troopers, the shallow depression he followed behind the river ridges so windless that the rising cloud of dust hung thick enough to make the Gray Horse Troop seem like a gap in the hurrying column. The clothing of the men, even the blue-gray trousers, darkened with sweat under the soiling. Lather burst from the laboring horses, some beginning to lag—for all the bloody spur rakings across the ribs, lagging and falling far back. Those with Custer on earlier Indian chases feared a violent explosion from the commander as the horses gave out, the sunken flanks like bellows, heads hanging toward wavering knees, some going down flat. But this time the colonel didn't even look back when his young brother Boston was off and trying to whip his horse back to its feet, the scouts passing him there, their smaller ponies running very hard to keep up.

Gradually a far sound of bunching gunshots thrust itself above the pounding of hoofs on the baked earth and through a low place the troops caught a momentary sight of the dust-filled river valley. Vague specks that were riders raced through it, the sharp cut of far carbine fire following the puffs of blue powder smoke. A cheer broke from the troops, the recruits letting their excited horses get out of control, some plunging ahead of the commander.

The colonel rose in his stirrups and shouted after these men, "Hold your horses, boys! There are plenty Indians down there for all of us!"

Then Custer touched his spurs lightly to Vic's lathered sides and led out in a gallop again, dodging behind the higher ridges, out of sight of the enemies in the valley. More horses played out, not only those of the green men but that of Sergeant Finkle too, dropping him back from his position close to his captain, Tom Custer, back to where the Crows and Mitch Bouyer were whipping along.

Sergeant Kanipe, on a stronger horse, was up close and so received the call to carry the commander's orders instead of Finkle. "Go to Captain McDougall," Tom Custer instructed. "Tell him to bring his pack train straight across country. If packs come loose, cut them and come on. Quick! There's a big Indian village ahead. If you see Captain Benteen tell him to hurry up."

Then, as if to emphasize the urgency, the captain repeated, "A big Indian village . . ."

Kanipe turned and with his neckerchief drawn up over his mouth and nose he spurred back along the trail. The column started ahead at its fast gait. By this time Adjutant Cooke was back in his place from the river with Keogh where they had watched Reno cross and then charge toward the Indians kicking up the shielding dust with their ponies.

As Custer rounded a big bend of a hill, the firing off to the left was suddenly louder. Motioning to Cooke, he led toward the edge of a high point in the river bluffs and looked down upon an Indian village circle where only women and children seemed around, and exclaimed something that the Italian trumpeter, Martin, thought was, "We caught the Indians asleep," but was more probably that they had caught the Indians napping. Even that would have been a facetious remark, for Custer was visible to some of the men on the river bottom and so he could surely see Reno's skirmish line bloom into puffs of blue in a hot fight, with the haze of smoke and dust over hundreds of milling, charging Indians, and the horde creeping up that Reno could only suspect.

Custer jerked off his wide, light-colored hat and gave a cheer. To his men he shouted, "Hurray, boys! We'll get them and as soon as we have them we'll go back to our station."

Then he set his spurs and turned right, off the ridge that was ending against the river three-quarters of a mile down. He headed along the back of the second rise and across the point of a draw that cut the broadening slope to the river a diagonal mile away, with more villages plain on the far side. As the Indian scouts and Bouyer had warned, there was no ford for some miles below the mouth of Ash Creek, where he had been expected to cross in the support of Reno. But there was the dust of charging warriors at these lower villages too, and more Indians hurrying up from below and now some coming from above, too, still on the far side of the river but looking, gathering, signaling with mirror flashes and flapping robes.

The colonel stopped, Cooke beside him. The adjutant motioned Trumpeter Martin up and started to give him verbal instructions. "Take this order to Captain Benteen—" but then he pulled out a notebook and laying it against his leg, wrote the message to bring the packs.

With the note buttoned into his shirt pocket, Trumpeter Martin started across the three–four miles of ridges to Ash Creek, the way Kanipe had gone. The courier looked back from a rise and saw the command headed into a low, wide gulley in three sections, the middle one Smith's Gray Horse Troop, almost lost, like a gap in the line, still nearer to the color of the bald knobs and the rising dust. As they galloped on, the column swung leftward a little as though to strike diagonally for the river and the camps beyond. Martin heard firing behind him and glanced around. Parties of Indians were suddenly at the flank of the column and ahead of one section, too, afoot, as though rising out of the ground, some whooping and waving buffalo robes to stampede the horses, some shooting.

They had been hidden in ambush, waiting.

Martin tried to hurry faster, spurring his worn horse already panting open-mouthed, head dropped, stumbling at any clump of weeds or loose stone. A little farther on he saw a man coming toward him on a hard run: Boston Custer. He had managed to get his exhausted horse back to the pack train and replaced it with a fresher one. He slowed down to shout this and to ask Custer's location. Trumpeter Martin grinned, pointing back over his shoulder toward the gunfire, and young Boston hurried on, eager not to miss the best of the fight.

When Martin passed the point where Custer had stopped to look down into the valley of the Little Bighorn, he saw through the increased dust and smoke that Reno's force was surrounded by hundreds of Indians, the troopers falling back.

There was no time to watch, for now the pack train and Benteen had to be found in a hurry. Besides, some Indians saw the courier and they might try to intercept him.

Ever since the morning sun came to stand on the heights east of the river the scouts of the great Sioux camp were reporting soldiers in the country, but no one would have believed that they were so close and would actually attack in daylight, or even dare to ride against the vast Sioux conference at all. Then suddenly there was dust rising above the river crossing, and bluecoats charging in double file across the bottoms against the Hunkpapa lodge circle—soldiers falling into Sitting Bull's camp as his vision in the sun dance had foretold. By then the warrior society policing the camp that moon hurried out to whip their horses into the second wind for a good fight, and to raise a protective dust. In the meantime other Indians were running to help. Drummers hurried out to spread the alarm, mirrors flashed pale signals from the veiled sun. The one-feather men, members of the Teton council, hurried from the great lodge in the center of the three-and-a-half-mile stretch of village circle, the Hunkpapas Sitting Bull and Gall whipping to their camp, all the war leaders working desperately to prepare for the attack, to save the women and children helpless before the coming soldier guns. At the great conference lodge the guards stripped the painted skins from the eighteen-foot poles, rolled them up in sections, and, loaded on pony drags, whipped off westward to hide the skins in draws from the eyes of an enemy.

Back at the villages, criers ran around the lodge circles shouting that every young man was to get his horse and his weapons. The war chiefs were already riding through the camps with their bone whistles and their chantings, even in the villages far down the river, the Crazy Horse Oglala Sioux and the Cheyennes. Some men didn't wait for their fighting horses to be brought in from the prairie but took any mount available, whether the handsome ceremonial horse tied behind some chieftain's lodge or an old travois mare to be whipped into the fight. In the meantime the women ran gathering up their children and the trophies of their warriors while the older men directed their escape, whether temporarily or for a long flight if that should become necessary.

Then the two Reno troopers on their runaway horses had come charging into the Hunkpapa village and were brought down and cut to pieces. But their coming—that they could penetrate the strong warrior line—scattered the women and children running for the river, to swim where they must but to get to the east side, put the high-banked stream between them and the enemy. Then they saw the Ree scouts on that side, and so they fled downstream through the thin brush, women, any woman, dragging children by the hand, the babies on their backs bobbing hard.

The young Indians who were herding a few village horses in the pockets against the steep bluffs east of the river found themselves helpless with only their bows against the gun-armed Rees. They fled for the brush and the rushes too, letting the scouts sweep away the small bunches. But some of the warriors attacking the soldiers on the bottoms heard the shooting. Leaping their ponies down the river bank, they cut back part of the herds and hurried the Rees on with their guns. By that time swarms of war horses were being whooped in from the high prairie west of the river and soon the soldier fight was moving back toward the Little Bighorn.

As soon as the shooting was gone from the timber and across the bottoms, travois poles came rattling and jumping over the rough ground behind the old mares gathering up the wounded to be hurried to the medicine men. There were many to be carried away, for the soldiers, cornered, had fought hard. Women who lost men in that fighting ran out to avenge them on the bodies of the soldiers and the scouts, particularly Bloody Knife, with his Sioux half-sister there to help. His head was cut off in the ancient manner of the tribe, the custom long before they learned about scalping from the warriors who had gone east to fight in the French and Indian Wars.

While there was still the thunder and roar of a fight at the river and along the bluffs, Indians, mostly boys and older men, hunted the brush of the bottoms for live soldiers, and the dead too, to strip bare. Suddenly a man from the Cheyenne camp raised a cry. He was holding up a blue shirt with the 7th Cavalry insignia on the collar tab. This he had seen before, on the soldiers who had killed his mother and his wife on the Washita.

"This day my heart is made good!" he shouted, tears running down the grooves of his dusty face. Waving the shirt like a captured banner, he whipped through one camp after another, crying his news all the way to his own village, the farthest down the river.

But before now another messenger had come riding through the villages and on to those searching the bottoms, his arm pointing off across the river and beyond the bluffs that pushed against the stream. He was shouting something about more soldiers seen, many, many more—a long string of them riding along the far side of the hills. Instead of going to help those first ones, those being driven in a hard fight across the river, the column of bluecoats was heading along the second ridge and probably for the crossing near the lower Indian camps, where so many of the helpless ones, the women and children, the sick and the ancient, had run. But as they, too, saw the new soldiers, they turned back across the river with their children, shouting of troops even when the blue riders were still hidden from the camps.

"More horse soldiers are coming! They are on the sacred hill of the wild peas!" the women shouted.

It was true that troopers were riding over the little hill that was all in bloom, the recumbent loco weed like a painted robe under the feet—white, pale pink and lavender, rose, vivid magenta, and deepest purple. The long row of bluecoats on sorrel horses, and gray and brown, was crushing the flowers into the gravel—flowers that had always ripened to a mat of buffalo beans for the women to gather and boil in the meat kettles. Now enemies rode there on the hill of peace, come against them in plain daylight, coming along the pretty hill that had never shielded anything larger than the ant and the little gray jumping mouse, the horses cutting the bloom with their iron hoofs, their manure defiling the sacred place where youths went for their puberty dreams.

Suddenly the bluecoats broke into a gallop, the forked-tail flags ahead, the double row of riders followed by the long dust that rose from behind the hills—more soldiers riding hard to fall into the camp as Sitting Bull had envisioned.

Those around Reno at the river and along the bluffs couldn't see Custer, but four Cheyennes who had been hunting the bottoms for injured warriors were halfway to their own lodge circle at the north end of the great camp when they heard the alarm of the new enemy coming. They pushed their horses down the steep splashing jump into the river and climbed dripping out the other side. From there they moved in a formal row around the point of the river bluffs and up the open slope of ravines and draws that fanned out from the far, high ridge where the dry heads of the two Medicine Tail Creeks started. Bobtail Horse led the Cheyennes, all four singing their death songs and shooting their weapons, mostly bows, lifting the arrows into the air toward the troops, who were like a row of far trees against the grayish sky. They were too far away to hit, but the Indians hoped to slow the string of soldiers hurrying along the broken heights that turned toward the lower part of the Sioux camp and ended in a point across from the Cheyenne lodge circle. The cloud of women and children who had fled there were running again, away from the new danger. The older men led them up the low rises to the left of the river and out upon the gullied prairie, to scatter there like quail.

From up the stream, hidden by the first line of ridges, rode Gall, the Hunkpapa, with Crow King beside him, their followers strung out behind. Gall had been leading a charge to cut off Reno's retreat to the bluffs with the fierceness of a wounded grizzly, the man wounded, too, in his most vulnerable spot: his wife and children dead in the Hunkpapa village. But one of Gall's warriors on a high point had signaled to hurry down the river. Another, a bigger, bunch of soldiers was riding fast against the lower villages and had already crossed the dry little valley that was South Medicine Tail Creek. Turning in fury, Gall whipped his horse along, his mourning tatters flying out behind him, his rifle across the withers of his lunging horse, ready.

Other warriors were hurrying across the river now, many putting their horses over the steep river banks, then to vanish into the ravines. Seeing these things, Custer's Crow scouts lagged more than ever, their horses worn out or deliberately held back as they had been on the hard run from Ash Creek. Finally the scouts stopped on a high point and looked, dark-faced, toward the great Sioux camp and then to Smith with his Gray Horse Troop going down South Medicine Tail and Custer hurrying along the slope northward—the scouts just sitting, making no words.

Mitch Bouyer reined over to the seventeen-year-old Curly, the handsome, wavy-haired Crow breed.

"You are very young," Bouyer said to him. "You don't know much about fighting. Go back, keep away from the Sioux, and go to those other soldiers, there at the Yellowstone. Tell them all of us here are killed."

Curly looked down upon the spreading dust of the warriors, warriors of the Sioux, that most powerful enemy of his mother's people, gathered here in such numbers as he had never seen before. Although their war whoops were still far off, the sound carried easily against the barely perceptible wind. He looked over the river once more, and then kneed his stockinged, bald-faced pony into a run southward along the still-dusty trail. From a high point he peered back under his palm. Bouyer was riding toward Custer, who had halted the command to let the men tighten the saddle girths for a hard fight. Then the colonel led off diagonally across the head of upper Medicine Tail ravine. Many Indians moved along the bottoms now, some openly, more hidden in cuts and draws and washouts, ready to rise.

The young Crow turned his horse off deeper into the hills and struck out for the Yellowstone and General Terry. He swung far around the Sioux attacking where Reno was digging in on the hill, and around Benteen, coming up along the bluffs from near Ash Creek.

The other three Crow scouts still with Custer had warned him as sternly as the Rees and Bouyer. All of them had said flatly three days ago that the enemy would be too many, far, far too many. Now, seeing the Sioux camp strung for miles along the river and the warriors moving in spearheads up the slopes, the scouts stopped again, stony-faced, holding themselves aloof, plainly with no further concern here; and so they were told to go, get out.

"Save yourselves!" Mitch Bouyer called back as he kicked his horse into a run to overtake Custer, angrily forging ahead without his Indian scouts.

Once the Crows stopped to watch the colonel's command for a moment. They saw Smith and his Gray Horse Troop trotting diagonally across the ravined slopes, gradually thrust sideways by an occasional bullet spitting up earth and gravel around them, the horses jumping back as from rattlesnakes or rearing and plunging as the sting of the lifted arrows sent them sideways into the dust of the company ahead, higher up the slope. Together the Crow scouts kicked their weary horses into a dog lope toward the lodgepole trail along Ash Creek five miles away, circling far around the Sioux coming from the back of Reno Hill. Judging by the hard fire they had heard against the major, all his men must surely be dead by now anyway. But Benteen saw the three scouts and signaled them over to help dig trenches with their long knives, at least for a while. They came, their faces sullen, but they came, dodging the Indians left hidden to keep these troops pinned down for a later return to the attack as one held a buffalo herd until the hunters were ready. The finish here would be easy; the troops on the hill were exhausted, encumbered by many wounded and by empty cartridge belts.

The warriors from the Reno fight rode against the new soldiers with the power of victory in them, their paint furred with dust. Some had bloody scalps at their belts, some with blue shirts on their backs and captured carbines in their hands, perhaps even with cartridges heavy in the pipe bags or breechclout flaps tied up for pockets, the two warbonnet men proud that no bullet had come through the feathers to reach them.

While the Indians from the east and northeast of Reno Hill

went along the back slope of the heights toward the spreading dust of Custer's men, those from the river side of the bluffs were led by Gall in a swing low down around on the left, to cut the troopers off from the river and the camp circles beyond. The warriors farther down were crossing anywhere, many at the pony ford near the mouth of Medicine Tail Creek, some to spread upward, like the sharp, raking claws of a hungry grizzly reaching up for a row of small and imprudent mice along the rise. The Indians slipped into ravines or cut banks or washouts, mostly leaving the horses hidden, creeping in upon the enemy. A few did charge boldly in the open, but not in the usual single recklessness against which Crazy Horse, Gall, and others harangued. This was not the day for mere coups and honors, as in wars far from the villages and the helpless women and children. This day they must strike hard, strike to destroy this enemy who dared attack their great summer conference, something that had never happened before. No army had ever come shooting against a Sioux camp of any size except upon the band of Brules under the peace chief, Little Thunder, twenty years ago. For that, too, there must be punishment today.

Some of the more daring of the young Indian women, boys, and older men gathered on rises to watch the soldiers who had stopped their horses in a long, segmented row strung out for three-quarters of a mile along the heights. They watched the officers spur together up there with gestures and shouts, arms pointing toward the river and the Indian camps beyond, field glasses turned upon the warriors streaming along the slopes. Some of the young Indians went up closer now, whooping, waving robes, stinging an occasional horse by a lucky shot, to plunge and rear.

Now there was a hesitant stopping and starting in Custer's movement along the high backbone to where the ravines of the main Medicine Tail started. He led down to the dry gullies and across toward the ridge that ran parallel to the river, about half a mile from it. More Indians swarmed over the stream, and from above. They swept some of the horses of the rear troops against those ahead, against the Grays, while more warriors came up toward the rugged ravine that led to the nose of the ridge ahead of Custer and still clear of dust.

The first solid return of fire by the troopers was from the saddle, and brought two warriors down and several Indian ponies, driving the foremost warriors back for better cover, to snake themselves forward again, up draws, from bank to sagebrush. They dropped arrows among the soldier horses, soon too excited for steady aim or for a good stand, plunging even from the whoops and the waving blankets of the occasional daring young Indian eager for coups, leaving here and there an empty saddle, the trooper hit or thrown. Then suddenly the pale sunlight glinted on shining instruments held to the mouth as a group of Smith's Gray Horse troopers blew a battle song. The sound cut clear and thin over the far valley and the farther ridges, perhaps to hurry the pack train and Benteen, if the captain hadn't obeyed Custer too closely and was not too many valleys away.

The fine sound startled the Indians a moment and brought young women riding out of their watching places. Then the warriors saw that it was like their own battle songs, and they began shooting again, the soldier horses rearing and running. The trumpets were hastily replaced by carbines spitting rows of new smoke. The Indians did not break and retreat, and many of the soldiers dismounted, as Calhoun's and Keogh's troops were doing against Gall and his warriors moving along the slopes from the southward, and those behind them too, now also from the Reno fight. Every fourth soldier held the horses and tried to take them to protected ravines and gullies, but not too far away, while the men, both on the rise and down the slope, fired from the knee for careful aim or what was hoped would be careful.

Indians were hit in the repeated volleys, but more came in the growing charges, some riding on horses captured from Reno, with blue coats to get up close. Finally the soldiers began to go backward, retreating up the slope, helping two wounded men along, trying to make little stands, not only to hold the enemy back, but to keep the troopers who had never fought whooping warriors from breaking into a run that could not be stopped. The Indians on the river side signaled those behind the ridges for cross fire, safe for the warriors, with the troops on the backbone above them, the few bullets whistling overhead. They were determined to prevent any from escaping, as Crook's men had managed to withdraw at the Rosebud eight days ago. But Crook's horses were not tired out and his infantry had their good long guns, his force altogether, so many more than here. Besides, these looking down into the valley of the Little Bighorn had come against the women and children and must be punished hard, punished for that as well as for attacking a Teton conference.

Lieutenant Sturgis with a platoon of the Gray Horses had moved into a deep gully leading toward the river, perhaps to locate a crossing; but almost at once Crazy Horse and his followers pinned them down, the Indians anxious to protect even the poles of the great conference lodge from the first enemy attack against it as well as to keep the shooting from the helpless ones. Creeping up, the warriors lifted their arrows to fall among Sturgis' men and horses. The gully walls were cut and broken, and it seemed the inexperienced young second lieutenant might hold out until the Indians were driven back. But elsewhere the troopers were retreating, some no longer kneeling to shoot or even leaning forward against the kick of their guns. They just fired and ran, each soldier trying to get to his horse, ready to flee. Most of the animals were wild with terror now that the steadying hands of the troopers were failing them. Some plunged back, rearing, going over backward in their panic even with seasoned troopers, the best, finding their guns jerked with the finger in the trigger guard. Some of the troopers hurriedly rein-hobbled their horses by tying one rein short to a forefoot. These the warriors charged whooping through the dust, particularly the Cheyennes with Lame White Man from the Reno fight, leaving the troopers little time to untie their horses or even to cut the leather, so that some fell still reaching for the rein, the gut-shot horses screaming, the stink lost in the stench of powder.

By now the shooting was hot from the back of the ridge where Calhoun's men were trying to make a stand, the dust and smoke so thick that it was hard to tell a trooper from a warrior. Only two men were plainly visible. One was a soldier left behind in the small retreats, his horse played out, the man brought down by arrows and a war club as he ran, his shirt dark with blood. The other was an officer boldly riding back and forth trying to direct the fight and hold the men firm. It would have been a fine coup to pick him off, but always he seemed to be lost in the dust as the sights came upon him.

In the meantime Gall's warriors were moving in large numbers toward the knob held by Calhoun. Those afoot worked their way up the slope. Jumping high in the haze of the fight to let their arrows go and then dropping down out of sight, they drew soldier fire and a waste of soldier ammunition. The bold officer was still riding around there in the dust and smoke, trying to rally his men. Finally one of the many whose aim was upon his horse brought it down, to stagger up again; but the man had sprung to another mount as agile as any young Sioux set afoot in a war charge. He rode on but somebody got the brave one at last, because suddenly he was not seen any more.

Farther back, Gall and the judicious Crow King massed their mounted warriors and drew in several other parties. When the high, thin call of Gall's war flute cut through the roar of the fight, the Indians rose together with a great whooping. Those afoot worked like sharpshooters while the mounted warriors whipped their horses into a charge that carried them clear over Calhoun's men, the shouts and cries of the troopers only empty mouths working as the horses were upon them, the war clubs swinging, leaving dead and wounded scattered behind. But a couple of important Sioux went down too and, infuriated, the warriors charged on northward to Keogh's men, getting some who hadn't scattered out to run along the ridge toward Custer. Even then they had trouble turning their excited war ponies far out in a swing back to the slopes. But good warriors had been left behind, unhorsed, perhaps, and flattened like trembling cottontails in the scraggly scatter of grass and sagebrush, but with the shielding dust and smoke to sting their eyes and lungs. The wounded and the dead were to be dragged away, sometimes by a rope around the pony's neck, the end tied to the belt of the warrior's breechclout so the running animal took him out of the fight, dead or alive. More often it was some bold relative or friend or warrior brother charging into the fight to carry him off.

By now the riderless horses breaking away from the soldiers had stampeded in every direction, some running toward the stock of the troopers along the ridge ahead, toward Custer. Most, even the wounded still able to run, fled down the slopes, many with reserve ammunition untouched in the saddlebags. The loose horses were caught up by youths and young Cheyenne women coming across the river. Several of the tribe, including two of the women, rode through the thick of the battle darkness clear up and over the rise where Custer had passed on his way toward the point of the ridge that ended half a mile from the river, and not much farther from the Cheyenne camp. The fighting, too, had moved out along the narrow backbone, and the young riders passed unchallenged among the scattered dead of Calhoun's and Keogh's troops looking for wounded Indians. On the way one of the young women swung off leftward close to the fighting along the slope where her husband was leading an attack. She fired a few shots with her pistol and when the soldiers made a small countercharge, she carried off a young Indian whose horse was killed under him. With him behind her she whipped her pony away through the stinging murk and the whine of carbine bullets.

The dust and smoke thickened over the almost windless battlefield, so dense and shielding that the troopers, driven toward Custer's position, were fleeting shadows as they ran, mostly afoot, dodging from dead horse to hollow and weed, hurrying on toward the head of the column or going down, face in the torn gravel. But the same battle darkness hid much of the concentration that was closing around the men in the cuts and ravines between the nose of the ridge and the river and closing around Custer Hill, where a scattering of troops from the heights were gathering. But their commanders, the Custer brother-in-law, Calhoun, and Custer's favorite, Keogh, both lay dead on the far rise. Keogh, who had come out of the Foreign Legion and the Papal Guard to a ridge in Sioux country, lost one of his side whiskers there, stripped off as an unusual scalp.

With ocasional glimpses of the thousands of Indians swarming up from the river and along the slope, and no telling how many creeping up close for a sudden overwhelming, it is improbable that George Armstrong Custer remembered his remark a few months earlier: that his 7th Cavalry could whip all the

Indians on the Plains. There was desperation now, and the bravery of desperation. Suddenly a lone rider with three stripes on his sleeve, Sergeant Butler, spurred out of the dust over North Medicine Tail ravine and started across the slope, riding hard through breaking clouds of smoke, straight into groups of startled Indians who let him disappear, perhaps thinking for a moment he was an Indian in the clothes of a trooper he had killed. But realizing who he was, they charged him, whooping their signals of an enemy fleeing. Butler shot back a time or two, although mostly he clubbed his horse along with his carbine, straight ahead, determined it seemed to get through southeastward, probably to the pack train or Benteen or to carry the message of disaster to the outside, to some telegraph office that Custer had hoped to reach himself before another day. The sergeant covered over half a mile through bullet and arrow but on an open slope he was finally brought down, the Indian who killed him praising his bravery in song.

Back behind Sergeant Butler, Lame White Man was leading a strong force of Indians, mostly from the upper camps, against the troops of Yates and Tom Custer while more Sioux were creeping up to the siegers holding the Gray Horse troopers in the deep gully. Lame White Man had had a good day and was wearing a blue coat he found tied behind the cantle of a captured saddle. But in the battle clouds over the slope it was difficult to recognize anyone and so the bold war leader from the Southern Cheyennes was killed by a Sioux who thought he was one of Custer's Indian scouts.

Lame White Man was soon avenged. His followers, doubly furious now, made repeated charges against the troops in the ravines, killing or stampeding what seemed the last of their horses and then charging them, afoot and mounted, until all were dead or running for the last hill, Captain Custer, Yates, and even Smith of E Troop fleeing too, the officers somehow

mostly still with horses, Mark Kellogg with his mule, he to fall
not far from the circle at the top of the ridge. Boston Custer
and Autie Reed didn't make it to the hill but fell on the slope
from the river. An officer on a sorrel horse was the last to retreat
toward the hill. A Sioux wearing a scalp shirt rode at him and
was killed, and then a Cheyenne. Brave Bear was the third, but
his bullet brought the officer from his horse.

In the meantime Crazy Horse was leading his Oglala Sioux
up the slopes in one attack after another until his horse began
to fail. Then he swung back to his village for a fresh battle
mount. From there he rode down the river leading many Sioux
through the Cheyenne camp past the lodge of the Sacred Buffalo Hat, the holy object of the Northern Cheyennes. The little
tipi was open, the Sacred Hat surely carried out upon the
prairie for safety from enemy contamination. More and more
warriors on fresh horses gathered to Crazy Horse as he crossed
the river with the drumming back among the helpless ones
throbbing like spring in the ground to his ears. His Winchester
ready in his hand, the Oglala led his warriors around the end of
the Custer ridge, heading toward the ravine behind it to cut
off the escape he feared, particularly since he lost Crook's men
last week. As Crazy Horse rode, more and more Indians came
up behind him until the fresh war horse was the point of a
great arrow, growing wider and longer, the dust of it joining the
cloud standing like a thunderhead into the sky.

They reached the upper ravine just as the Indians from the
river side pushed the soldiers up to the end, the nose of the
ridge. With a great whooping the fresh warriors charged the back
of that blue stand, using mostly arrows, spears, and clubs, hot
for the close combat. The roar of the soldier guns seemed little
more now than the popping of the winter ice going out of the
Yellowstone in the spring. In the wild riding attack the ponies
jumped a Sioux who fell among them, jumped him like so much

sagebrush or stone. The first charge by the Crazy Horse warriors broke over the top of the ridge and circled the troopers on Custer Hill, the cluster of men fighting from behind their horses, dead now, the warriors cutting off any who might be fleeing there from the slopes. At the next charge a few Indian horses were hit, another man or two, nothing to count in this fight of a summer day on the Little Bighorn to protect the great conference lodge and the helpless women and children. Hundreds of warriors circled and charged and circled again, more than hundreds, clotting together in the dense smoke and dust from the battle whose roar was deafening to the ear in a darkness as of evening.

There were some good men on that hill, some still trying to shoot carefully from the knee even as the Indians closed in, but the circle was getting smaller, men piling up behind the dead horses as their carbines stuck, the roar of their revolvers choking in their hands. No Flesh killed the standard-bearer and tore the banner from his faltering hand, while another bold warrior rode straight through the little circle of troopers, his pony jumping the dead horses and men. He was followed by a whole charge, and so the soldiers went down under hoof and spear and war club until it seemed nobody could be alive in that bloody pile. But there were a few. Jumping up together, they headed off through the haze of smoke and dust down the slope toward the brush of the river, so very far away, the whooping warriors running them down like newborn buffalo calves, striking them to the ground, looking for more, until suddenly there were no more.

While the warriors sat around on their horses, not believing this easy victory, two young Sioux came back from the breaks, disappointed that the fight was over so soon. They had chased an officer who escaped in the smoke on horseback and were cheated because he put his revolver against his head and all they got was the killed-himself one, and couldn't even strip him, as a suicide. By now even the horses here were gone, all rounded up down along the river. The animals had been so worn out they were not afraid of Indians, as trooper horses usually were, but just stood, heads down, as the youths came to gather them up, and the women passed, some with travois, some singing victory songs. Spreading up the slope, they ran over the battleground seeking out their dead and wounded, keening as they found the dead ones, avenging themselves on the bodies of troopers nearby, stripping the white men to the skin.

Next came hundreds of boys and youths riding out to the battlefield to sit their horses and think about this victory that was already bringing alarm to the faces of the headmen over the punishment to come. But who was to punish the great Sioux nation? the foolish boys asked each other. Many of the youths had found carbines and revolvers or were loaned them by relatives to fire volleys into the dead soldier bodies, as in the old days they would have shot hundreds of arrows. When every brush patch and washout had been whipped through for hiding troopers, the war leaders rode back to the ridge of the dead. By now they were stripped, naked and white as buffalo fat where the clothing had kept off the sun, looking so pitifully weak and helpless. These were the men who had killed so many women and children, the Cheyennes told each other in wonder.

But they had killed no helpless ones except Gall's family, not on this day long to be remembered.

Now the warrior societies formed in individual lines and, crossing the river, charged into their villages shooting, whooping, singing victory songs, to be met by the women who had fled to the upland with the small children, all running back, only now feeling safe. But some at the upper camps looked uneasily toward the knots of troops on the ridges across the river. Still, they sang their warrior welcoming songs.

But there was the uneasiness among the councilors, those who knew something of the white man's numbers, and even among the war chiefs who feared the day of retribution when they had so few arms and so little ammunition while the soldiers had the roaring wagon guns, the cannons. Some pointed to those soldiers up on the hill, still alive, the ones who had struck first against the great camp and killed even Gall's stepson besides several good men. Those soldiers must not escape either, and so, with whoops and battle songs, the leaders headed the thousands back toward Reno, and saw that those soldiers had all moved out and were bunched at the edges of some high points like lead buffalo cows smelling out a changing wind. Plainly, they were also as blind as the buffalo and would be as easily scattered as those soldiers already dead, and would die so easily.

In St. Louis, as the later Democratic delegates were gathering on the afternoon of the 25th, New York's Tilden seemed to be strongly favored over General Hancock; Hancock to become another soldier-president if he won. But this time he would be the responsibility of the Democrats, who had been howling about the corrupt administration of a greater, if Republican, general. Yet surely the high tide of anger that had been raised against a soldier-president could be diverted. There was the popularity of the romantic fighters against the Indians, and while General Hancock was not the dashing figure of a Custer, he also had burned a Cheyenne village.

Yes, if Hancock came up as a dark horse and the circumstances were just right, he might win the nomination, if no more attractive figure appeared.

Three days before the opening of the Democratic Convention there were the usual last-minute scandalous rumors, this time against New York, the state's Colonel Church charged with having "some unhappy pecuniary relations with a female descend-

ant of 'The Father of His Country,' " followed by the antici-
pated public brawling between the pro- and anti-Tildenites.
There were rumors, too, of something brewing among the
Michigan delegates, without a suggestion of its nature. The
New York *Herald* carried an editorial on Crook's defeat:

> Some time ago we knew of certain regiments going into the
> Yellowstone region. Why they went is not clear. . . . Critics
> of the administration will say that if General Grant had not
> removed that superb Indian fighter Custer to avenge Belknap,
> we should not now be mourning ten dead and twenty
> wounded soldiers. . . . He (the Indian) has been plundered
> and starved. We have hunted him as a bear or a panther.

June 26, the *Herald* asked "Is Hancock the Dark Horse?" although the paper was still speaking for Bayard. June 27, more
corridor brawls were reported and the *Herald* complained about
"The gallant Custer in the role of a guide" in the search for
Sitting Bull.

Anyone in St. Louis expecting the triumphant telegram from
Custer that the colonel had hoped to send abroad to the world
had to receive it no later than the 28th.

»▶ »▶ »▶ »▶ »▶ »▶ »▶ »▶

6 RETURN
TO THE
SIEGE

★ ★ ★ ★ ★ ★ ★ ★ ★

Under the thin gray streaks of dust and smoke, so high they seemed a part of the whitish mare's-tails across the sky, some of the Indians still sat on their horses in scattered little knots along the slopes. They had been looking off northward, firing an occasional gun in their victory exultation. Then there was a gesturing back to the soldiers coming along the ridges and finally the stopping to look. At a whooping and a rough, wavering blast from a trumpet, the warriors wheeled their horses, first here and then there, to start in prongs up the ravines toward Reno's hesitating groups of soldiers on the far points. The fighters from their victory charges through the villages came too, crossing at the pony ford near the mouth of Medicine Tail Creek, or, impatient, spread out along the river, leaping their horses from the bank, throwing water high, and, clambering out, whipped up the steep bluff sides. They cheered and whooped each other on, for if those soldiers up there ahead died as easily as the ones left white and naked scattered along the open, unshielding ridges and slopes down the river they might miss the fight altogether.

"Nobody is to be reckless and get hurt. The soldiers can all be killed by no water," the war leaders cautioned in one way or another. But the young warriors were hard to hold. Sweeping toward the soldiers, they began firing their new guns and ammunition, although some were a mile away and more, some swinging out to cut off the nearer, the bolder, and more foolish of the troops. Captain Benteen watched them come. He had moved out beyond the rest to a point where he hoped to see some sign of Custer and his battalion. There was only the thin spread of dust cloud and the warriors moving along the slopes, but across the river, villages were strung out as far as he could see, perhaps 1,800 lodges and certainly hundreds of the small wickiups for the young men—at least four or five thousand warriors.

By the time Reno and a small detachment reached the high point farther on than Weir, he could see swarms of Indians— thousands. The major told Adjutant Hare that their position was not a good one to make a stand, not with the Indians beginning to pour into the shallow gorge that led up behind Benteen and behind Weir's men, too, and the scattering of other troopers, gathered in dark little rims along the edges of the ridge points. Plainly the command must be consolidated, and quickly. As the roar of guns came closer and closer, even Weir, in spite of his partisanship to Custer and Reno's orders to open communication with the colonel, had to see the danger as his men began to waver before the bullets that sent the horses, particularly those of the recruits, plunging and rearing, wild to escape.

The small knots of troopers began to fall back from the various points, following Reno's lead. He was hurrying, with Moylan's wounded and the pack train to be protected. Benteen planted a guidon on Weir Hill when he passed, as a signal and a guide and cheer to any scattered men or detachments who might come in sight. French, who had already felt the Indian charges on the bottoms and to Reno Hill that afternoon, was retreating fast, too, and so Weir fell in behind him, the troopers spurring and whipping the worn horses. When they neared Reno, Weir sent Hare to report that he had found the whole country ahead of him covered with Indians and that they had been getting around his position.

As more troops fell in behind the common retreat, Edgerly of D Troop was trying desperately to mount his frantic horse, wild from the whoops and the shooting, with several Indians charging in from the sides. He made it just as the first warriors came up over the bluff within rifle range but riding flat against their ponies, difficult to hit by the troopers shooting back on the run. The Indians aimed mostly for the cavalry mounts, not to kill so much as to graze, drive them wild to escape their riders, who could be cut down with war club and ax, the horses rounded up by the herders. One trooper was wounded in the saddle but clung there while several others were set afoot, running through the dust and smoke to catch a stirrup or even a flying tail. One of Weir's D Troop slid to the ground and lay there, bleeding. As Edgerly passed, he called out to the man to get to a hole and he would form a skirmish line and come back to get him. When Edgerly managed to reach Weir to tell him of the promise and ask for a line, the captain refused. Orders were to get back to the hill of the earlier stand.

It was true that the Indians, on their fresh horses, were gaining fast, sweeping down the saddleback and up toward Reno Hill. Godfrey saw that such close pursuit would throw the whole command into confusion and fright, perhaps start a real rout, particularly among the men who had already had their units decimated by the power of the Indians that afternoon.

With his fresh troops dismounted and deployed, he made a stand to cover the retreat. Lieutenant Hare, on the way back from Reno, who was hurrying on to his hill with Moylan's wounded and the pack train, decided to stay with Godfrey, even though he was the adjutant and perhaps needed elsewhere. With the Indians sweeping around toward both sides of Reno Hill, Godfrey sent the led horses ahead to the command, while his troopers flattened into small depressions and behind clumps of sage and gumweed to slow the Indians, shoot some down so the rest would hunt cover. But although his men brought some of the horses down, the warriors clung to the far side until they actually fell and then slipped into the charging Indians, to be dragged away, the thundering mass of warriors no thinner but sweeping in by the hundreds—the thousands, it seemed—so that Godfrey was ordered to fall back rapidly while he could. Keeping up the firing, the troopers ran, stooping low under the dust and blue puffs of smoke from bank to weed to hollow, falling spraddle-legged, ready to fire. Bullets struck all around the men, spurting dirt and gravel over them, the *ping* overhead ever more demoralizing.

When they reached the ridge before Reno's position, they found the men there dismounted and being set around the shallow depression, the horses and the pack train corraled and a picket line thrown out, mules tied to it and unpacked. Dr. Porter gathered the wounded in the bottom of the shallow hole, protected as much as possible with pack saddles set in a barricade around them.

It was a well-maneuvered retreat, as the experienced Plains soldiers like Benteen realized, with only one man lost, although there were wounded to add to those fevering and thirsting from the earlier fight. In spite of their own precarious situation, several of the officers, and the older troopers too, talked among themselves about Custer.

Perhaps he had had an encounter and withdrawn to the Yellowstone and General Terry . . .

But mostly the men worked fast to prepare for the attack to come, surely planned to overwhelm them, ride through them. The Indians already darkened the heights and began to sweep down in hard charges that called for staunch defense. Finally they surrounded the hill entirely, the firing general all along the line, very fast and at close range. The Ree scouts who hadn't started for the Yellowstone hid behind the east ridge, watching. Some of the warriors saw them and took up the chase. The Rees scattered and flattened to the earth. The Sioux, afraid they would miss the fight and the plunder on Reno Hill, gave up the search, and when they were gone Young Hawk climbed to a high point where he could see Reno's flag far off, along the river ridge. He cut a stick, tied his white handkerchief to it, and with the Rees gathered up, several afoot, but the wounded on horses, Hawk led off to Reno. They met a lot of Sioux swarming up around back of the ridge and had to run. The soldiers saw the scouts coming and began to shoot too, past them into the chasing enemy. Near the hill the Hawk's horse went down but, still waving the white flag above him, he raced for the troops, through the continuous roar of the attack on Reno. Panting, Young Hawk fell into the little hollow, grabbed a hardbread box, and flattened himself behind it while the wounded Rees were dragged down to the little breastwork protecting the other injured ones, and where a keening went up at the news that Bob Tail Bull was dead.

By this time the outline of Reno's position was roughly a wide circle, with the southeast, the upstream, side cut off flat and open. This, Reno ordered closed by some of Mathey's hardbread boxes set in a low barricade, making the whole defense line an irregular horseshoe, with the end barred. The ground fell away there for some distance, but with a high point beyond from which the Indians dropped arrows and bullets into the depression.

Benteen had left one company back on the ridge to hold it at any cost, but when the Indians struck those troopers, they came running in as fast as any others. He sent Captain Godfrey's men to another rise to hold the Indians off as long as possible and ordered Wallace to place his troops in a weak spot. Wallace pointed out that he had only three men left in his Company G, and was sent anyway, with a promise of support. He would need it, with at least 2,500 warriors surrounding the command, the firing hotter than the troopers could be expected to face for long.

Reno was making the rounds of his defense and Benteen fell in beside him awhile, the two men moving stooped down as they talked. The show of a hat or a head or anything lifted on a gun barrel brought a volley of arrows and bullets through the slow-rising smoke. They directed the tightening of the defense line. The horses and pack animals were corraled more securely in their circle, the reins of a dozen tied together and anchored to the legs of dead horses. Moylan's company covered these from behind the pack saddle breastworks Mathey had set up for the wounded. To Moylan's left were Weir and Godfrey, then French, Wallace, and McDougall, with the latter's left resting on the downriver bluffs. On the upstream side Benteen's line stretched along a higher knoll offering a farther sight area and, consequently, farther exposure. By then it was about five-thirty in the afternoon, perhaps later. No one had time to look at a watch, certain to be on Chicago time anyway. As the firing sharpened, every man hugged the dry, dusty earth, making himself as thin as possible, none with the time to dig in if there had been more shovels, those flattened down behind sagebrush hoping that it was neither transparent or bullet-welcoming, the whole command—particularly Reno's battalion—in no condition for hard work or for a protracted wait without dozing off in the desperate need for sleep.

The Indian circle around Reno's position was about 4,000 yards in circumference, the warriors at varying distances, from knots of headmen observers at 1,200 yards to warriors as close as 30 feet—young warriors making records for great boldness before they were detected and brought down for their daring, but not before they took a heavy toll, their memory to be honored in song and story.

Somehow the Indians seemed to have more guns or ammunition than down on the bottoms, good guns that carried far. The troop to the right of French's Company M lost several men, killed within a few minutes by fire from a high ridge. One of the Indians seemed to be a genuine sharpshooter. French's men saw this and flattened even closer to the earth, waiting their turn while they tried to spot the culprit in spite of the Indian's usual quick jump away from the betraying spread of his gun-smoke. Yet for all the attempts to stop him, the sharpshooter worked into M Troop and down along the line. He killed the fourth man from Sergeant Ryan, hit the third and struck a second, who jumped back down among the wounded to the doctor. Captain French and the sergeant, both certain that Ryan's turn was next, leaped up with half a dozen of their men and instead of firing straight ahead as before, they wheeled suddenly to the right and put a deadly volley into the heights, and while they could not see any effect through the stinking smoke, the Indians ran and the sharpshooter fired no more.

Gradually the sun receded and dusk came. Now the red spurts of gunfire exposed the exact point of discharge, but creeping Indians could move up close without detection through the shadowed low places almost within spear's reach of the troop line—spear and arrow that created no betraying fire. The situation looked more and more desperate. Darkness was coming fast, to cover united charges that could surely overrun the thin circle of soldiers. There was perhaps more confidence against this possibility in men like French, Moylan, Benteen, and Reno, who understood the Indian's conviction that fighting after dark was bad luck, a survival from the old days when night dews not only softened the moccasin sole to the rock and the thorn but—worse—stretched the bowstring so it refused to send the arrow into the darkness.

The firing slackened as the clouded night fell, sometime between nine and ten o'clock in that region, but there were signs of sentinels left to guard the besieged soldiers, with the frequent sound of hoofs on the hard earth, sound of horsemen coming and going. Even half a dozen creeping Indians could be a great menace to troopers who had had almost no real sleep the last three days, with hard, weary marches and bloody fighting. The younger men particularly fell asleep at the first lull.

Several times Reno tried to get a detail to water, but the Indians were most watchful along the river bluffs, with piles of dry grass ready to blaze up at the least sound or movement, exposing the creeping troopers to the pitiless glare, and the bullet and arrow.

The men of responsibility on the hill, as well as the packers and other civilians, wondered about Custer, with no courier from him, no signal by day or night. Many believed that he had probably been defeated and driven down the river. Yet his horses were worn out, with even Boston Custer having to return to the pack train to replace his. The Indians, as all who had seen the great moving herd knew, had endless horses, tough and fresh, for relays in the chase. Still, Custer, wily and known for fool's luck, probably had his men with General Terry this minute, to return to the Little Bighorn with him; instead of Custer meeting Terry and Gibbon coming up the river tomorrow evening or the next day, when Custer's whole force was to be in from his scout, then with all the 7th Cavalry alive and well.

But mostly the troopers thought about Terry because even tomorrow might be too late for them here, and no telling what Custer reported to the humoring general if he did go there. Benteen and some of the others remembered the desertion of Elliott on the Washita, even the bodies unrecovered. Who could say why he didn't trouble to support Reno as promised? There were several men here whom Custer could spare from his regiment without much regret.

It was a time of bitterness, of darkness not entirely of the night. Besides, some knew of the promise Custer had made to Bloody Knife: that a victory over even half a dozen Sioux lodges would make him the Great Father. Who could say what small camp might have been discovered by the Crows or Bouyer for Custer to destroy, and that he was not hurrying a message to a telegraph station this moment for the Democratic Convention gathering at St. Louis?

By now the question, "What is the matter with Custer?" was receiving increasingly impatient replies. Whatever else tomorrow or the 27th might bring to the men besieged on the hill, there would be hordes of howling redskins around them before dawn, and now was the time to prepare for the attack, prepare as well as could be managed. And if anyone forgot, there were the little red glow spots of enemy scout fires reflected against the clouds overhead, fires of Indians watching them on every side, with occasional hoofbeats of horsemen coming and going, perhaps relief for the sentinels, with now and then a wolf howl or an owl's hoot that the scouts and the old-timers recognized as entirely too natural—surely Indian signals.

During the evening fight it was planned to send a messenger

out as soon as possible after dark. He was to locate Custer or go on to Terry coming up the river, deliver a paper telling of their troubles here. Forked Horn agreed it should be done, but he was a Ree and unfamiliar with the region. Unfortunately, Goose, a Crow who knew every gully and badger hole within fifty miles, was wounded. Anyway, several couriers should be sent out, mounted on the strongest government horses remaining, all to ride hard, pay no attention if any of the others were shot. Both Reno and Varnum of the scouts emphasized this: one of the men must get through. Anyone who fell wounded was to pull out the message paper so any soldiers who might find him would see it.

At a scout's suggestion, the farrier removed the iron shoes from the horses so they could run better, Forked Horn said, with less noise or sparks from stones, and leaving no tracks behind to betray them as soldier couriers for any skulking Sioux. With best wishes but without trumpet blast or fanfare three Rees, including Young Hawk, Custer's favorite meat broiler, started. At the last, Goose, even though wounded, insisted on going too, for he knew the country, Goose and a white sergeant. They eased their horses cautiously out along the darkness of the ravines, but it was not like a man creeping. The Sioux heard and fired on them, so they all whipped back.

Reno, weary from the hard marches and the three bloody encounters of his men with overwhelming forces in one day, was very disheartened. He tried to get some of the civilians who knew the country to carry a message out. They refused. Varnum himself volunteered, but Reno pointed out that the lieutenant had no knowledge of the region, so even at best it would be suicide. He could not let a man with no chance at all go out. Perhaps toward dawn they would try again, when their Indian scouts were more inclined to travel, less certain of bad luck in anything of war in the nighttime. But they were all of tribes who understood the power of the Sioux, and preferred to stick close to the little hole on Reno Hill.

The older campaigners knew that Indians were notoriously close-fingered with fuel; but as the night darkened, the fires in the villages across the river blazed up high, even those far out of sight casting light against the thin clouding overhead, the figures dancing around the nearer flames making gigantic leaping shadows in the light that flared up against the bluffs and ridges along the river where Benteen's men particularly could see them. Desperate for rescue, it was easy for the fevering wounded to imagine columns of troops here and there below, and others too. Once, many thought they saw the shadowy duskiness of troops moving over the hills and ridges, with the dull thud of iron hoofs, the command of officers coming from far away, and even a proper blare or two of a trumpet. Stable call was sounded by one of Reno's trumpeters, shots were fired in signals of friendship. Every hope possible gave itself form: a civilian packer leaped to the bare back of a horse and galloped along the line in the darkness, shouting.

"Don't be discouraged, boys!" he kept repeating. "Crook is coming!"

Crook . . . the only general who had ever succeeded in an attack on a substantial village of these northern Indians, and then not the Sioux but only a part of the small tribe of Northern Cheyennes. But he had struck and destroyed the village out of a cold dawn last March, not in the heat of summertime and not against the great summer conference of the Teton Sioux. There would have been even less optimism if the men in the circle on Reno Hill could have known of Crook's fight up the Rosebud eight days ago. It had required only part of the gathered warriors to drive back General George Crook, the graying Indian fighter, and with a much stronger force than the entire scouting regiment, Custer's 7th, all together.

Soon it was plain that General Crook was not coming, nor anyone else; and gradually the men, even the frightened romantic recruits, had to give up their dream of a storybook cavalry rescue and start digging rifle pits as fast as they could in the baked and stony earth, working in groups of threes and fours through the danger of creeping figures in the dark and the unusual amount of howling northwestward from wolves under the thinner, higher, more hysterical yip and cry of the coyotes. At the start Benteen had sent to the packs for spades, but there were none there. Sergeant Ryan of French's M Troop had a couple of small ones and in addition used boards from the hardtack boxes for digging. A few of the troopers had hand axes and hatchets, others used their knives and even the forks from their folding mess kits, as well as tin cups and halves of battle-punctured canteens.

Reno made a hurried round of his position, stumbling into the fresh holes in the darkness, and over legs sprawled out. Worried, he was driving the men, knowing that dawn would bring a concerted attack beyond anything his force had yet endured, even those who had been on the bottoms with him. There was some talk of slipping away, secretly in little groups, and openly, the whole command going, even leaving the wounded behind. But with the worn men and animals and the Indian watchers to signal any movement, ready to bring overwhelming pursuit, it could only end in a disastrous running fight or a stand in a much less defensible position than here, and with no water anywhere or even the hope of it. Reno moved cautiously among the dusky figures of the wounded where Dr. Porter worked by touch, with even a momentary matchlight bringing swift bullets. The blood and woundings were already a sweetish stench, some of the men talking wildly, begging for more water than the mouth-wetting from the lightening canteens being saved for them. Several were no more than boys, city boys away from home in a wilderness teeming with Indians and thirst and pain.

When the commander came to the packs protecting the wounded and the animals he found a great many skulkers there, some packers known through the regiment for their thieving and some other civilians too, perhaps thinking they might as well take now, for there might be no tomorrow, puncturing the few tins of canned fruit with their knives, drinking the juices—juices and fruit Reno was trying to husband for the wounded through what might be days of siege. He had already fired Girard, missing since the fight on the bottoms but not considered dead by anyone, such were his wily ways. Reno had thought he was stealing from the government and refused to sanction his employment further. Now the commander drove the packers and the other civilians away from the supplies, but he had to return to do this several times, finding packs broken open, half the contents gone, particularly the fruit. Roaring out that the horses and mules were safe and did not need these men, who had no business there now, Reno demanded of one of the more troublesome what he was doing among the packs and received an insulting reply. This, on top of all the day's trials and sorrow, infuriated the commander so he struck at the man and shouted out what many said was a threat to shoot him if he was found among the government goods again. Benteen was angry too. He had had to drive some of the packers from the goods at the bivouacs all the way from Fort Abraham Lincoln, drive them out like thieving dogs.

As the night drew on, the fires flared higher in the villages along the river, with a roaring of songs and drumming pierced by yells and gunshots. To those who knew the Indians this

seemed a lot of victory-dancing for Reno's soldiers lost—even
for Bloody Knife, the traditional enemy who had led Custer
into the sacred Black Hills two years ago. Besides, he had
brought the soldiers here to their summer conference, after it
was driven away from Bear Butte by the miners that his guid-
ing had tolled to the place called Deadwood. Still, there seemed
excessive jubilation in the vast Indian camp, even counting the
two troopers whose panicking horses had carried them into the
Sioux village, the village of Sitting Bull, the man whose dream-
ing had been pictured at the sun dance site back on the
Rosebud.

"Soldiers falling head first into his village . . ." the Sioux
scouts had said the signs meant.

Some of the troopers less schooled in Sioux warfare thought
of prisoners being tortured in the camps, as in the old stories
of the Iroquois and French Indians flaying and burning their
captives two hundred years ago. True, some of the Sioux remembered their early custom of decapitating their enemies,
the heads carried through the victory-dancing and then impaled
on the poles of their fortified villages in the upper Mississippi
country. Inkpaduta and his small group of Santees who had
fled to the Tetons after the troubles in the Spirit Lake region
were probably the only practicing decapitators in the camp.
Lieutenant Hare and some of the others did recall Lieutenant
Harrington's gloomy foreboding that he was to be captured and
tortured. Back early in the expedition he had made sketches of
himself tied to a tree with naked savages dancing around him.
It seems he sent these back by mail courier, not to his wife
but to a friend, and yet he had not been easier in mind.

There were several light sprinkles during the night, the rain-
drops making light running sounds over the dry earth, like
timid mice. But there was not enough to wet one parched
tongue or to soak the grass piles of the Indians watching the

way to water. Besides, there was repeated heat lightning, revealing all the ridge and its bluffs in rosy glare. Toward dawn, ammunition and rations were distributed for the coming fight, dry rations with not even alkali water for coffee, the whole-bodied, too, suffering from thirst although the Little Bighorn was only three–four hundred yards away.

Relays of short rests had been arranged, some of the troopers sleeping while the rest dug rifle pits or built breastworks with the boxes and the bags of bacon, hay, and oats. Pack saddles were set up in rows, some with pads and blankets hung between them, offering protection from the eyes of the enemy when dawn came if not against his bullet, arrow, spear, and even knife and tomahawk, for it would surely come to that if the command was not relieved soon.

Only Reno seemed not to rest or even to nap. "Great God, I don't see how you can sleep!" he told Edgerly on the lieutenant's awakening.

Toward dawn the fires and noises of the villages lessened so that Benteen's men along the bluffs could see the interlacing of fireflies in the valley below and hear the fall of the arrow hawks upon their flying insect prey, a peaceful night sound as though there were no men dead below them, and none still to die not far away. Several times the Indian scouts and the old plainsmen put a naked ear to the ground to detect faraway sounds of regular hoofs—cavalry or even Crook's infantry marching—but there were only irregular vibrations, perhaps a little late dancing below, and surely of Indians coming and going from their guard points.

With the first graying in the east around two-thirty or three there were two rapid shots from the Indians splitting the dark sky together, apparently a war signal. Some of the troops were still digging when the attack opened and sharpened as the light silhouetted the tops of the ridges. Spits of fire revealed the

Indian circle, with puffs of powder smoke spread almost imperceptibly in the pale light, followed by the lagging boom of the farther guns. They were answered by the troops, but with caution now, many of the wildly shooting recruits of yesterday's fight on the bottoms either dead or grown into veterans in twelve hours. All the men of the circle except the side against the Little Bighorn had some shelter as the light crept down over them, at least if they lay flat and kept their heads down. But Benteen's men were guarding the broken canyons and ravines that led from the river directly to the bluff top, into the entrenchments. To watch these cuts and breaks the men had to expose themselves and gradually some managed to slip away under the smoke to Reno's hole, to hide among the packs. Benteen went to run them out, his voice harsh with dust and fury. He made them drag down some of H Troop's pack saddles, bacon bags, and hardbread boxes for a redoubt to protect his wounded until they could be moved to the hill.

As the east grew lighter and reached in reddening streaks up the clouded sky, it spread a flush over the gray, dusty men on the hill and then moved down the slopes and finally over all the bottoms. Down along the river, morning fires sent twists of smoke out on the prairie where horse herds were sweeping in from the western upland. Indians gathered in swarms along the river—mounted, warrior Indians, apparently reserves waiting for space in the attacking circle. Buzzards hovered over the Reno bottoms, drawn by the dead men and the bloating horses. Some were flying off northwestward too, most of them beyond clear view even with the field glasses, disappearing, dropping down out of sight as several eagles soared in fast and high, like swift bits of black hair against the graying clouds.

The attack sharpened, the Indians drawing all the fire they could, to wear out the ammunition and make the cartridges stick in the heated carbines as they had done yesterday, but there were ramrods from both the supply packs and willows cut by some of the old-timers on the bottoms. Here and there warriors poked up mats of dark buffalo hair on the end of their guns or their coup sticks, buffalo-head mops, with feathers stuck in them, like the top of Indian heads. The bolder ones jumped up high and dropped down, drawing the fire of the recruits who believed they could guess where the men would drop. In the meantime a small knot of sharpshooters gathered on the high point out of range of the Springfield .45 carbines, using infantry rifles mostly captured from Crook last week. They hit the horses and mules in the shallow depression, setting them wild, their empty saddles flapping a little, the Indians hoping to stampede the stock out across the prairie, young warriors ready to round them up.

Benteen's men also suffered from these guns, with their section open to the long-range firing from the northward too. After a long roaring of shots from all around, the flashes paling in the brightening day, the mounted charge that all experienced Plains fighters dreaded came. With their horses whipped into a high run in their second wind, the warriors clung flat to the heaving sides as they headed straight for the little circle on the hill, hundreds of Indians it seemed, firing. In spite of the warning to keep cool, take careful aim, some of the Indians got clear into Reno's defense line before they were turned aside. Some were dropped, perhaps the horses going down headfirst or slowing, stumbling. Others ran free, their riders gone, perhaps to be dragged away by the neck rope tucked under the rider's belt or carried off by a fellow warrior.

As the advance scattered in the dust and smoke, the officers hurried among their men, here and there one hit, perhaps in the head, finger still on the trigger, to be lifted out of the way before the next charge. By now Benteen realized that his position was the key to the whole defense and that he would probably receive the next onslaught. His ammunition was getting very short, some men down to four–five cartridges, and no relay of boxes possible to them over the exposed bluff crest that was in the sights of Indian sharpshooters. He was disturbed, too, by his growing number of wounded, who could not be moved to protection or to Dr. Porter, still working without sleep to ease and comfort the desperate condition of the injured now that the water was gone. Yet if the Indians made a determined rush, retreat of Benteen's troops was inevitable, with the collapse of the entire bluff line and the probable loss of his disabled, perhaps all of Reno Hill and the men dug in there.

Ordering Lieutenant Gibson to hold on, under no circumstances to fall back, Benteen, under such cover as his best marksmen could give him, slipped up a shallow ravine to find Reno. He discovered that all the defense was hard-pressed, with earth and gravel spurting up over the defenders, the whine of bullets ricocheting from pebbles and rock loud above the thud of lead on flesh and the sobbing of some of the wounded. He found Reno up at Weir's position, lying low, his head once more covered by a dusty blue kerchief, lifting up now and then to survey the area and ducking as the shooting multiplied.

"The Indians are doing their best to cut through my lines and it will be impossible to hold it much longer," Benteen reported to the commander.

Reno pointed out that the whole defense was in great danger, but when Private McDermott came snaking up a cut under the smoke, bringing Gibson's report that the ammunition was almost gone, Reno had to consider the problem. Unhappily, the fight was growing even hotter all along the line, the bowmen becoming very expert in raising arrows high to fall among the horses and the wounded. Still, he could not afford a breakthrough from the river, so he ordered Captain French with his M Troop over to the southerly side. He and his men at least knew something of the terrain there, from the retreat.

On the way back, Benteen, his curly hair powdered with gray dust, gathered up some more men from the horse detail and hurried down, just in time. The fight was almost hand to hand now: a hundred men, it seemed, against every one of Gibson's, all ready to charge in upon them bodily. One warrior shot a trooper from so close that with one plunge forward he touched the body with his short coup stick. The man was killed by an alert trooper and lay there in his dusty, bloody paint and breechclout, the only Indian casualty left in sight anywhere because he was too close for even the most daring rescue. The warriors moved around, but there were always some on high points out of range, watching and directing, generaling the fight by signals to the many hidden behind ridges and cut banks and in ravines two hundred to five hundred yards off in a continuous circle around Reno's command, at one place sometimes less than thirty yards from the troops. After the hot exchanges the Indians seemed to think the besieged were so hurt and disorganized that it was the time to charge again. They came once more, under the smoke and dust, sticking flat to their horses, those afoot dodging from ridge to hollow to weed, perhaps arching their silent, unbetraying arrows into the soldier hill.

By now there were no spoken questions about Custer, only a rare meeting of eyes and a bitterness worse than alkali on the cracked and blistered lips.

French agreed that the men scattered around the bluff face, unprotected, visible from at least one side or the other or from below, must be kept there at any cost. Benteen wanted the Indian boldness repaid with a charge of the two companies. Reno slipped down to lead it, the firing a roar of steady thunder, the smoke clinging to the breaks as the troops moved afoot, creeping, running, falling. Somehow they pushed the warriors back from one protective ravine and draw to the next, some almost to the river. But the Indians had endless reinforcements to take the places of their wounded and dead as a counter-charge was built up.

The attack was costly in ammunition to Benteen's men and in casualties. They were gathered to the shelter of a ravine, all but Private Tanner of French's M Troop. He was hit far out on an exposed knob and unable to drag himself out of arrow shot. At a hurried call for volunteers Sergeant Ryan grabbed a blanket from a saddle and with three men ran to the wounded Tanner, rolled him upon it, and, stooping low, with bullets and arrows, even a spear or two striking around them, the flying gravel sharp against their faces, got the man to the ravine of the wounded. In a few moments Tanner was dead, but it heartened the men to know that their injured were rescued as daringly as any Indian.

Captain French's favorite horse, the best buffalo hunter in the command, was among the held ones near the wounded men. The animal received a long-range shot in the head and began to stagger around, setting the other horses to rearing and plunging, trying to break loose. Private Voight of M Troop started to lead him out of the way and got his brains spattered over everything, as Bloody Knife had down in the bottoms, when Reno stood beside him.

Soon the firing commenced in greater fury, most recklessly from the southeast, evidently to cover an attack gathering else-where. Reno gave Benteen permission to make up a short charge from D, G, and K Troops.

At the captain's shouted order, "Give them hell! Hip, hip! Here we go!" the men leaped out, carbines ready to fire at will.

Only one man stayed behind in his little pit, crying like a child. In their run over the ridge, Benteen's men could see

a large body of Indians gathered at the foot of one of the hills
to the north. As the short foot charge moved toward them,
firing as the men came, the Indians broke and scattered. All the
troopers returned. The only serious casualty was the man who
had remained in the rifle pit, crying. He was dead, apparently
by a bullet from his own pistol.

By now the men on Reno Hill were ordered to keep down,
to save themselves and their ammunition, for they must somehow last until Terry and Gibbon arrived. It was the first real
admission that Custer was no longer expected to join them.
The men flattened down low in their shallow holes and
trenches and behind dead horses, the buzzing gases in the heat
bloating the bellies up high until hit by bullets. Any that struck
bone released not only a terrible stench but blew the rotting
flesh over the men hid behind them. Even less fortunate were
the troopers lying beside corpses swarming with flies, those dead
since yesterday bloating like the horses, with maggots beginning to work in the blackened mouths and eyeballs, the sight
even more horrible than the stench.

The horses and mules up around Dr. Porter's patients were
so wild for water that their rearing against the picket lines endangered the wounded men unable to escape. Even the horse
guard was liable to injury, the number doubled for safety, although the Indians were driving holes in the outer line. The
whole command was desperate for water, the thirst aggravated
by the sultry heat of the summer day where the thermometer
often went above 110 degrees. The occasional spatter of rain
running over the grass was only a tantalization, the smell of
water driving the horses to wilder plunging. Even so, the dust
was never laid, gritty and burning in the dry mouths of the able
as well as the burning and delirious wounded. The men were
forbidden the comfort, and the drying effect, of a smoke or a

cud of tobacco. Some put pebbles into their mouths; some tried to chew grass. Those whose hunger drove them to gnaw at a little hardbread found that it blew out of their mouths like flour in their breath. A few raw potatoes offered a little relief, but there were so very few. Several times volunteers started over the bluff rim for water and were always driven back or left flat on the broken earth. Now and then a recruit who would be a hero slipped away without authority—none of those who had been on the bottoms with Reno: they knew. Sometimes the daring one got back through a costly cover of bullets to hold the eager Indians back, and face the scathing, dry-mouthed profanity due a fool in war.

Benteen, with the best view of the river and the bottoms, estimated there were two thousand Indians around the hill and as many as a regiment waiting along the river for their turn to enter the fight. A formal file of Indians on good horses, a couple of the grays almost as well matched as Smith's, came to watch from a remote point. In the center group was a white-patched golden buckskin that the troopers with Custer in 1873 declared belonged to Crazy Horse. Whoever the Indians were, they gathered, with the horse heads close, apparently in consultation, and then dismounted and settled in a circle for a smoke, with signals from mirror flashes, bannered spears, and hands. It looked like a concerted charge was coming, the depression on the hill to be overrun by the very number of the enemy. But apparently it was put off, for now the warriors in the attack no longer exposed themselves, although a few got close enough to send rocks and spears into the circle by hand and to count coup on a dead trooper within Benteen's line. They dropped arrows into Weir's and Godfrey's men too, and had to be driven out by a charge like Benteen's once more led by Reno. There was a suspicious lack of real resistance and after the troops were withdrawn the Indians slowed their attack, apparently waiting for the thirst to do their work, as the troopers told each other sourly. No use losing more warriors.

By now most of the men on the hill had had no water for sixteen hours, the horses for twenty. Dr. Porter came stumbling with fatigue to say he must relieve the thirst of his patients. His wounded were dying, more from the lack of water than from the injuries. So the desperate attempt must be made; somehow they must reach the river. A skirmish line was arranged, to be put out as soon as there seemed some hope of success, Benteen ready to offer all the protection he could give to the water detail. A party of volunteers draped with empty canteens and carrying camp kettles crept out, to run from rock to bush to bank into the steep ravines that led to the bottoms. But from there they had to make a rush across the open space to the river, much like the spot where Reno's men had suffered such casualties. Those who made it with the kettles dipped them and tried to race back to the ravine to fill the strings of canteens hanging from the carriers like vines of flattened fruit. Indians, hidden in a nearby brush patch fired on every man making the run. Some of the soldiers went down, their kettles spilling; others tried it a second time, with kettles spurting water from bullets and arrows. As the wounded accumulated, there was the additional need to rescue them, with more men endangered. But the water relay went on somehow, the smoke of gunpowder clinging over the brush and rising upward in parallel streamers, while the arrows from bushes and hollows left no betraying trail.

By noon the shooting up around the hill had quieted, the troops saving ammunition, the Indians probably stopping to eat and sleep a little as was their custom in even the hottest fight. But the river was still closely guarded and there were still sharpshooters on a high knoll, out of range of the carbines. One of the sergeants, handling a fifteen-pound .45 Sharps with telescopic sights, fired a few times to get the range and then put several bullets into the sharpshooters' nest to quiet them a little.

Sometime in the early afternoon an appalling number of Indians suddenly appeared out of the draws to make a fast charge all around the command. Leaving their horses out of range, they crept up and drove the troops down into their pits and trenches once more. Once more it looked like the end, this time by generalship. McDougall was ordered to make a little charge against the creeping Indians. He covered about sixty yards, until the firing got so heavy from the right and then across his position that he had to retreat.

But the Indians seemed to be withdrawing too. Reno came over to look.

"Where are they going?" he asked, peering under his shading palm.

"Downstream," McDougall replied, from what he had seen outside the depression, and fell into step beside Reno as he circled the line.

There were still small groups of Indians on the higher ridges, but some from the bottoms were trailing away downstream, too, leaving smoke to rise behind them from patches of grass and sagebrush, the smoke pearling upward. Slowly the Indians withdrew from the heights too, and those surrounding the hill.

An hour passed and another without more than an occasional arrow's fall, with no crack of Indian gun all that time. Gradually the troopers got up to stretch, wiping the dust and soot from their red-rimmed eyes, the dirt from their gaunt, stubbled faces. More men slipped down for water, creeping cautiously out of the ravine, looking toward the brush patches, some of them afire with a green-wood smoking and smudge. There was no crack of rifle or silent flight of arrow. While a detail helped Dr. Porter soak the stinking bandages from the wounded, the first smell of coffee brewing in the kettles crept over the weary men. Bacon was frying, perhaps on sticks over the coals, the hardbread catching some of the sputtering fat. The prairie fires along the bottoms had spread, moved off in the wind, leaving their black trail behind, but watched by few except the sentinels and the officers, out on points, looking.

By seven in the evening someone of the second relay of guards lifted his hoarse voice in an involuntary hurrah. From behind the trailing smoke, blown aside now and then, he could see an immense moving mass starting up the low breaks to the prairie on the west, the left side of the river, apparently heading toward the mountains. One after another the men forgot all danger and gathered in close groups on the ridges to watch under their palms, shielding their eyes against the late sun. Even the officers forgot the danger from skulking snipers left behind and passed the field glasses around. Although the movement was miles away, it looked like one of the vast buffalo herds that once marched those prairies; but they were all gone and besides this was not so dark. It was the great camp of the Indians in a solid, moving flow of riders and family travois with their lodges and belongings, the poles stirring up dust that drifted slowly away, curiously golden in the evening sun. The horse herds were along too, generally off to the side—many, many horses, probably the twenty or twenty-five thousand that the Rees had predicted would be there as part of the great Teton summer council with their usual allies and guests. The creeping blanket stretched out for miles, some thought as far as three or even five miles over the evening prairie.

"Thank God they gave up the fight!" someone said, and although "giving up" didn't seem quite the right words, almost anyone from Reno Hill might have said it, for certainly that many Indians could have overrun the hill any time they were willing to take the casualties, or they could have waited in safe and comfortable relays of watchers for the thirst to finish the work.

Then someone expressed the disturbing possibility that the Indians might just be short of meat and grass—very convincing in such a vast camp—and were moving the families to some buffalo range the hunters had located, the horses to fresh pasture. Afterward the warriors could sweep back to overwhelm Reno's command in close combat. For the first time the troops and most of the officers realized the full power of the Indians —enough warriors to overwhelm Reno's command with no more than knives and war clubs—understanding finally what the scouts really meant when they told Custer that the Sioux were too many, and the sense of Bouyer's suggestion to him: "Get your outfit out of the country as fast as your played-out horses can carry you."

It was true that the Indian scouts might have detected Terry and Gibbon coming up the river, but suppose that Terry did not come and the Indians returned; suppose that the warriors, all the warriors of so great a camp, managed to prevent the general's march up the Little Bighorn?

The dead men and horses in the hot June sun were drawing flies, carrion beetles, and some of the circling vultures from down the river. Reno decided that his command must move nearer to water, away from the stench and the health hazard, but to a position that could be defended if they were attacked again until they could retreat to the pits on the hill. The move was made slowly, well guarded and carefully, along the rugged ravine to assigned positions. The horse guard under McDougall was watering the frantic stock, a few at a time at the narrow pony ford, permitting only a half a dozen quick swallows, then to be whipped out to the grassy plots, most of the horses unsaddled for the first time in forty-eight hours, to let the animals roll in the dust. Later they were watered again and then a third time.

The rest of the men were caring for the wounded or digging pits and a protected area for the fifty-two who had to be carried very gently, with a couple of amputations necessary as soon as the doctor dared to perform them. For the present, they were all shielded from the sun's glare and the dust as much as possible, Dr. Porter, worn and without sleep, working to save lives that might still fall to an Indian war club or knife. By dark the eighteen men lost on the hill had been buried as properly as possible in the baked and stony earth.

That night Lieutenant De Rudio, Private O'Neal, Girard the loud-mouthed interpreter, and Jackson the breed scout came slipping up to the new position. Many had assumed that they had fled with the Indian scouts or even been killed, they and some other troopers who sneaked up too now. Several had expected De Rudio to look out for his own skin very well, and certainly Girard would take no part in any dangerous activities. He had the trader's instinct to keep out of other people's fights. The men all had their stories ready. Left behind in Reno's retreat, they had found it safer to hide in the brush up the valley, in the direction the fleeing scouts had taken.

Night sentries were set, some far out, trustworthy men, with frequent relief. Tuesday morning, June 27, brought reveille without morning guns and the first real meal for the men since the camp on the Rosebud. The stock was watered again, fed and rubbed down, the scalded and galled backs washed and treated. But Reno, the man of all the 7th Cavalry who had faced the most Sioux, was not giving up his caution now. He anticipated a possible trap and renewed his orders that every man be ready to take to the pits at a moment's command, even though the lookout with field glasses couldn't see an Indian, nothing except a few ponies grazing down the valley, apparently loose and deserted.

"The worst sign in Indian country is no sign at all," one of the old-timers offered sourly.

Trumpeter Martin sounded retreat, recall, and march, to draw in any of the command who might be hidden out somewhere. He went to the highest point around and blew his trumpet again, the instrument gleaming in the sun, blew it loud and clear to carry for miles.

There was a growing uneasiness about Terry. Where was the army? Could it have been held up, waylaid, ambushed by the men of that great moving camp? Or had Reno and Benteen been deserted as Elliott was on the Washita? Perhaps they should move out tonight while the region seemed clear, cut their way through; yet that might mean losing the wounded in a running fight. Still, for the moment anything seemed better than to wait for the Indians to return.

Although couriers had been sent to find Terry or Custer—at least Custer's trail—it seemed they had found nothing or they fell to the Indians. Then, midmorning, someone detected a pale cloud of dust streaking the horizon far down the river in the opposite direction from the Indian march. The trumpeter sounded assembly, the horses were put into the protected area, the kettles and canteens filled, and then there was nothing but more waiting. Reno, Benteen, and others went to high points to look through the time that seemed to stretch forever but was actually about an hour. The slow advance of the dust seemed proof of troops, including infantry. Surely no Indians moved like this, so it must be troops—but whose? Anyway, Lieutenant Wallace was sent out to show Terry or Custer or Crook how to get to the Reno position.

As the march neared, no one could pick out a Gray Horse Troop with the glasses, so it was not Custer's force, or Terry's either, for Custer must surely be with him by now. It must be Crook. Cheers went up for him, for old Braided-Beard, as the Indians liked to call him.

Then a white scout, Muggins Taylor, came spurring ahead to the sentinels who crowded around, barely letting him speak. He bore a message from General Terry to Custer, dated the 26th, stating that two Crow scouts had reported that the 7th Cavalry had been whipped and nearly annihilated. Terry had not believed them but was hurrying anyway, with medical assistance. The scout said he had tried to get through to Reno's lines the night before but the Indians had driven him back.

Yes, that was very probable.

By now Lieutenant Bradley of the 7th Infantry rode in asking for his friend Godfrey, who hurried up, demanding, "Where's Custer?"

"I don't know," Bradley admitted. "I suppose he was killed. We counted a hundred and ninety-seven dead bodies back there. I don't suppose any escaped."

Bodies! A hundred ninety-seven bodies! The command was dumfounded. It was not only the first intimation of Custer in real trouble, but even the first suspicion that he might not have escaped that overwhelming body of Indians.

The men hurried to Reno and his officers, carrying the news, some stumbling in their shock and weariness.

When General Terry arrived, his face grave, gray above the bearding, was enough to verify the news, the appalling news. With tears standing on his lean, dusty cheeks, he told what had been found.

»▶ »▶ »▶ »▶ »▶ »▶ »▶ »▶

7 THE
RENDEZVOUS

★ ★ ★ ★ ★ ★ ★ ★

Terry's march from the Yellowstone started uneventfully. The only immediate problem seemed the summer sickness of Colonel Gibbon, who had to be left behind on the *Far West* while the infantry marched on ahead. Still, Custer's 7th Cavalry was not due on the Little Bighorn from the long scout until the 26th or even the next day.

The real concern about the delays over Custer's return from the East all spring was not only about the command of the expedition out of Fort Lincoln but, less openly, the fact that General Crook, up from the south with his Sioux scouts, was in the field for months. He had a real advantage and would surely try to locate and destroy the enemy before Terry's force could contact them. It was, in a way, a race between two commanders of military areas—Terry of the Department of Dakota and Crook, head of the Department of the Platte. After the orders to attack all Indians not on the reservations by January 31, Crook's force had taken the field early and managed to strike a Cheyenne village in March; in the Department of Dakota everything was held up by Custer's eastern junket—Custer feted by the Northern Pacific Railroad and the New York *Herald* and offending his superiors by his hearsay testimony before Clymer's Committee in the Belknap exposures—and by further insubordination, with no one of Terry's command moving against the Sioux.

Custer's scout high up the Rosebud and over to the Tongue should reveal something of Crook's activities as well as the whereabouts of the Indians, but so far no couriers had arrived, not even Herendeen, sent with Custer particularly to carry back news of any Indians on Tullock's Fork. Terry had arrived at the mouth of the Fork the 24th and lingered the next morning. When no courier arrived, he marched a few miles up the valley, hoping to meet Herendeen. Finally the general stopped and sent Lieutenant Bradley with his mounted infantrymen farther ahead. The Crow scouts refused to go on—getting more and more agitated about the powerful Sioux—and Custer had been given all the white or breed guides, men like Bouyer and Jackson, who knew the country.

Terry and the four troops of the 2nd Cavalry that Custer had spurned at the Yellowstone four days ago arrived at the mouth of the Little Bighorn very late the night of the 25th and camped. The next day Bradley and his mounted men saw three Indians that the Crow scouts hailed as friends. The three sign-talked and shouted over the swollen waters of the river about a great battle on the 25th in which Custer and all his men were killed. Then they whipped their horses homeward, suddenly followed by Bradley's alarmed Crow scouts.

The desertion of the Indians added some weight to the story, and yet neither Terry nor Gibbon, both inexpert in Sioux tribal matters such as ceremonials, conferences, and great councils, would believe the Indians could gather enough power to involve Custer in more than an engagement. With the shoes of

Gibbon's infantry spurting up the dust, the column followed the Little Bighorn to about twelve miles below Reno Hill. As they camped for the night, hundreds of mounted warriors gathered on the benchlands to the southwest. Now and then some bolder youth raced his pony daringly between the bivouac and the river, but no shots were fired and by dark all the Indians were gone.

At reveille the 27th not an enemy was in sight anywhere. The column started out early, marching along the even bench west of the river valley while Bradley and his mounted men scouted the breaks and ridges along the right side of the stream. From a highish point they noticed strange objects scattered over the hills rising far ahead—buffaloes, probably an Indian hunt, the whitish carcasses, skinned to the tallow, the dark not yet touched. But curiously there was no movement, no butchering women and children running from one animal to the next, no men packing the meat on horses, no one standing guard.

Terry halted when the glasses showed the first signs of the deserted Indian camp—the Cheyenne village, the ribs of the wickiups and bare, gaunt lodgepoles like clumps of weed sticks in the hot sun. There were more dusky patches farther on, as though a great Indian encampment had stretched in scattered villages up along the river for miles. But not one twist of smoke rose in the air, nothing that could be identified as a movement anywhere, except an eagle flying, or buzzards dropping to the far ridge where it seemed there had been a buffalo hunt.

The column was moved down into the bottoms behind a detachment riding fast through the first deserted camp circle to search out any hidden enemy, stopping to examine a burial lodge or two standing firm and neat in the midst of chaos that signified swift departure. Inside lay men in full paint and regalia, warriors and chieftains plainly honored for bravery in a recent fight.

During the short stops some of the soldiers, particularly infantry men, managed to slip into the death lodges, grabbing whatever they could—moccasins, beaded shirts and blankets, quivers, handsome bows and lances, anything. Outside, they tried to scavenge a little through the great scattering of goods over the campground—brass kettles that no woman discarded without desperate urgency, dried meat, clothing, robes and blankets, even the scarce hoop iron for arrow points.

The horse droppings, the freshly worn pony trails to water from the upland prairie, were beyond anything Terry or Gibbon had ever seen, speaking of great herds, many, many thousands of animals. Through all this sign of an overwhelming force the column was kept moving in uneasiness, the old campaigners certain they were being watched by hidden Sioux scouts, with no telling how many of the warriors of this great camp might be waiting in ambush in some timber patch ahead, some narrow canyon.

The bearded Terry slumped in the saddle, his eyes alert, his dusty face sweat-streaked in the early-morning heat of the sun, the regimental colors sagging in the stillness of the air. On the ridge across the river a mile or more away, Bradley and his men were riding among the dark objects, going from one to the other, but apparently without haste, even dismounting. Some-one with Terry thought he detected another movement through the steadied glass—this one far ahead—a lot of dark specks on the bluffs also along the east side of the river, specks moving around but not marching, with no trail of dust rising, as over Terry and Gibbon's men, and no faint spreading haze from earlier travel hanging in the sky. Then three men appeared on a point across the river from Terry, apparently troopers in what seemed uniform through the glasses, and on cavalry horses. They were the volunteers from Reno, come to investigate this mass of men moving up the river bottoms with orders to escape somehow to Terry if it was the Indians returning.

By now Bradley, pale under the dust and sunshine, and silent, had plunged through the flooded stream and hurried to Terry. Saluting with parade-ground formality, he approached to report that they had examined the strange-looking objects along the hills to the east: 197 dead men of Custer's force, stripped to the bloated, discoloring skin, most of them unrecognizable, the dark objects their horses, all dead for days, two– three days.

A Terry scout out a long time searching for sign of Custer's force finally saw the three Reno troopers hurrying back to their command with the good news of Terry and Gibbon's approach. From the ridge the battle-worn men of Reno watched the column march up a little beyond the unburied dead on the bottoms, drag away a body or two and some horses, some already torn apart by the wolves, and go into orderly camp. Some of Gibbon's men were sent over to Reno's defense circle to skin the horses killed there yesterday, the hides to be dried for travel slings to carry the wounded down to the *Far West*. With no tents in the Terry command, men were hurried out to gather bundles of diamond willows for wickiups to be covered with blankets against the boiling sun of day and the chill of the night. The first shelters were ready for Reno's wounded by the time they were carried across the river to needed medical supplies and a doctor less hollow-eyed for sleep. One man of that first desperate water detail was suffering from a shattered leg whose spreading gangrene demanded immediate preparation for amputation when he reached the new camp.

Reno, gaunt and bristle-faced, remained to see about his wounded and then went to make a full report to Terry, from his first crossing of the Little Bighorn with Custer's orders to attack the great Sioux camp and his promise of full support. With their adjutants close behind, the men rode across the bottoms that had been grazed by the village horses of the Indian, the earth torn now by all the bare-hoofed charges of two days ago, the grass roots so cut up that the Indian fire had barely crept out of the dead rushes and timber patches. They paused at Reno's first stand and the ravine ahead of it, marked and scraped by the bodies of hundreds of men who had hidden there in ambush to toll the troopers to their death. They rode on to the Hunkpapa village not far below the ravine, where several blackened and burned lodges were left standing. Among these they located the mutilated bodies of the two men carried into the village by their stampeding horses, and finally the head of Bloody Knife.

Benteen got permission to take his troops across the battle-field to identify as many of the dead now, while it could still be done, and perhaps to understand something of the disastrous fight. He followed down the low gorge where it was assumed Custer had marched and was surprised that there was no deep trail, no trail of shod horses at all. Sergeant Kanipe moved off to Benteen's right, covering the ground he had crossed with Custer's message the afternoon of the 25th and seeking out the body of Sergeant Finkle who, but for his exhausted horse, would have been the messenger sent to McDougall, and Kanipe, still with Custer, would have died. As the troopers passed the points reached by Reno, Weir, and Godfrey the evening of the 25th, Benteen and some of his men stopped at the farthest of these heights, afraid to look ahead, afraid of what they would see, of what they might have missed then. But there was still nothing, no sign at all of combat, only the empty slopes where the knots of warriors had stood looking northward firing guns now and then against nothing—firing in victory as all the old campaigners should have understood. It was from there that the Indians had seen Reno's men gathered along several points and charged them, the warriors riding hard enough to cool even Weir's heat for battle, though he had not yet felt the force that Reno and his men understood.

The men of H Troop spurred across the slopes to a far, high

place, where suddenly the battlefield lay before them. It was like a great leaf, dead and fading in its straggly and browned June grasses and sagebrush, like a leaf crumpled into ravines and shallow gorges of dry waterways, with slopes rising along the ridges that were the broken midrib. Over the farther reaches lay dark objects—horses, bloated, the legs sticking out stiff as wood. Then they saw the naked bodies, in little rows, in knots and singly, dead men scattered like handfuls of pale Indian corn flung over a rumpled tawny robe in a children's game. There was no indication of battle lines or of orderly skirmishes except where five–six horses lay in a sort of string up a rise. Ahead of them were five–six dead men spaced about the same, as if they had run when the horses were shot, and were brought down too. They lay not far from Calhoun's body, all apparently running for the ridge that held one of the few clumps of troopers that had somehow gathered there and been brought down—perhaps twenty men killed not far apart—while off on higher ground, four–five more lay within twenty–thirty yards. But it didn't seem a stand, only a sort of sweeping together, perhaps with Indians creeping up the back slope too. The only real stand seemed on the far end of the ridge that pointed like a thumb at the river, below the last Indian camp. Here Custer had fallen with most of his officers within a barricade of dead horses, surely not killed so long as flight seemed possible, killed only in the last desperate moments to delay the end. Off southwestward in a ravine perhaps seventy-five yards from the river lay twenty-two bodies. Most of them seemed to have been killed with stones and war clubs. Perhaps they were the wounded taken there for protection, but more probably they had run there to hide, and were overwhelmed by warriors creeping up to the edge of the draw.

Benteen counted seventy horses and two Indian ponies dead on the field, indicating what every Plains campaigner knew: that the Indians usually fought on foot, crawling up, running, dodging, falling in protected spots, always free to grab any loose enemy horse. Riding over what was really a compact piece of bloodied ground, it seemed to the troopers that Custer's force had probably let their horses be stampeded in a panic of man and animal. The whole scene spoke of a rout, and a swift one, most of it lasting perhaps not half an hour.

Deliberately, Benteen returned to the nearest spot that any of Reno's force had reached the evening of the 25th. From there he and his lieutenant tried to see the battle slopes and ridges, and from the point where he had planted the guidon as a signal to Custer of Reno's position. The nearest of the dead was Sergeant Butler, a soldier of many years of experience and unquestionable courage. He was lying all alone on a slope, far from his company, as though he had somehow escaped at the last minute or been sent as a desperate courier to Reno, or more likely as a sort of final messenger from Thermopylae. But there was no miracle for him, and he went down with empty cartridges all around him.

Only three of Custer's officers were found with their companies, so apparently the fight was not by units. All but Keogh, Calhoun, and Crittenden were on or near the final hill near their commander or missing. Harrington's body was not with his C Troop, nor with his captain, Tom Custer, who lay up toward the stand made near the point where his brother died, nor found anywhere else. As the officers of the 7th talked this over, there were the uneasy recollections about Harrington's notion that he was to be captured and tortured, but close examination of the deserted Indian camps produced no sign of captives and none of torture, including no indication of the romantically horrible burning at a stake or tree that Harrington had envisioned in his sketch of himself.

Reno listened to Benteen's report, shaking his heavy head. He had sent both his striker and his cook to their deaths in his effort to get Custer to keep his promise of support. Perhaps he should have realized from the first the support would never come.

Early the morning of the 28th Reno ordered Captain McDougall and his B Troop to the Indian camps to search out implements to bury the dead. With what he could scare up—very little—the captain crossed the river in the bright morning sun. Someone noticed a movement in a small brush patch nearby—a horse. It turned out to be Keogh's favorite, called Comanche, with seven wounds but still alive. McDougall detailed a man to look after the animal and went on, as ordered, to bury E Troop of the Gray Horses—men he had commanded for years. Spreading his force out in a sad skirmish line, he moved up from the river, searching through hollows and clumps of sagebrush. They found them, most of the men dead in the ravine. From a distance it was plain they had used the upper sides of the cut bank as a sort of breastwork, sliding down as they were struck. Bloated and blackened as the naked bodies were—the faces like the wounds, puffed and swollen, oozing and flyblown—few were recognizable. The captain had a record kept of those who could be identified, pathetically few, although he had known many of the troopers for years. One definite identification was a sergeant because he had one sock on, with his name still plain.

But in the heat and stench the men trying to examine the decomposing bodies began to vomit so violently that McDougall finally had great chunks of earth and sod cut from the banks of the wide draw down upon the dead of Company E, covering them as well as possible, filling in much of the ravine's depth for all time, changing and obliterating much of the site.

Elsewhere, other burial details moved over the ground, men looking for some special friend going along, as Moylan went to see where Calhoun, his brother-in-law, lay. The bodies were all in similar condition on this third day of heat. Most of the dead were completely naked, many scalped and hacked, although it was no longer always possible to distinguish the wounds of actual combat from later mutilations. Custer's stripped body had been found in a sort of sitting position between two troopers in the low pile of dead behind the breastwork that was a tangle of stiff horse legs sticking out, and great bloated bellies, the gases stewing and whistling in the climbing heat of the sun, the rushing sound of maggots busily gnawing, great dark flies crawling heavily over it all.

Tom Custer's body was face down, most of his scalp gone except some tufts of hair at the nape. The skull was crushed, with several arrows shot into it and into his back. Godfrey had the body rolled over for identification. The features, pressed into the ground, were flattened and decomposed, unrecognizable, but on one arm, broken by a shot, were the tattooed initials TWC with the goddess of liberty and the flag.

There were 42 bodies and 39 dead horses on Custer Hill. Altogether, according to Godfrey's memoranda, they buried 212 bodies, bringing the dead, with the missing and those of Reno, to 265, including 16 officers, 7 civilians, and 3 Indian scouts. Without proper tools to dig the hard-baked and gravelly earth of the Custer ridge, the bodies were not buried in the usual deep graves or trenches. They were covered, but so thinly that those who knew the swift gully washers and cloudbursts of the dry country realized that some of the bodies would surely be washed out before fall, or covered by fill-ins beyond all finding, many of the poor markers set up at the graves of the officers certain to be swept away.

The men, ordered to destroy the Indian camp, to burn all that was possible, gathered up even the lodgepoles into rude blazing piles, the long ones from the conference lodge with the rest. They found the pocket instrument case of Dr. Lord, and perhaps realized that some woman must have been in great haste, leaving all those instruments with fine steel edges, sharp and keen, behind. The men also found the buckskin blouse of Porter, and some underwear with the name of Sturgis on it, both bloodied and shot full of holes. Young Sturgis' end seemed a particularly ironic one. Son of the colonel of the 7th with whom Custer had had a long-time feud, the young second lieutenant had been with Benteen at Fort Rice until two, three months ago. One of the lieutenants at Fort Lincoln was transferred East, and Gibson of Rice was offered the position. It was really a promotion but Gibson's young wife refused to let him take it, feeling an unreasoning foreboding against it. So young Sturgis asked for the opportunity to apply for the transfer and, perhaps because he was the colonel's son, although less than a year out of West Point, he was given the position, which put him into Smith's Gray Horse Troop on the Little Bighorn. Now Gibson was alive with Benteen, and not even a recognizable body remained of the son of the colonel.

Terry had planned to leave the battleground the evening of the 28th, but the doctors insisted that the disabled men needed another day of quiet and strengthening food before starting the long trip to the Yellowstone. The long, slow column started the 29th, when the lowering sun began to cool the broiling heat that had been so difficult for the wounded and the sick even in the shade of the wickiups. Each litter was carried by four men afoot, stumbling over the uneven prairie in the pale light of the growing moon. They had to stop every fifty or seventy-five yards to rest. The setting down and lifting was so painful that the carriers were doubled. After six or seven miles the command camped. Many of the troops went bathing in the evening river, but chiefly to slip back to the deserted Indian villages in the moonlight, and even to climb up to the stinking place where Custer's men had fallen, the fattening buzzards refusing to rise into dark flight, even the coyotes standing, looking, too lazy to run.

The stunned pall of the annihilation still lay upon the com-

mand, many of Reno's men and even Benteen's realizing the
luck of their battalions. There was quiet talk among the officers of Terry and Gibbon's forces too. What a difference the
2nd Cavalry would have made on Custer Hill, or Low's Gatling guns. Or abiding by the arrangements—to send Herendeen
to Tullock's Fork where Terry waited, Custer to scout farther
up the Rosebud and the Tongue and meet the command coming up the Little Bighorn on the 26th or 27th. Many of the
7th recalled the stern admonition of the scouts—the Rees, who
knew of the great summer council of the Teton Sioux and
said there were too many Sioux up ahead. Even the trusted
Bloody Knife had spoken with no more effect than the wind
over the buffalo grass, his headless body down in the brush
of the bottoms, the promise of a trip to Washington never to
be fulfilled. The words of Charley Reynolds had been unheard
as those of the Rees, as were those of Mitch Bouyer, both
dead now, and gone to their death knowing it would be so.

The next night the wounded were carried in mule slings
made of the horsehides, with the mules tied between the two
poles of each sling as between shafts, one mule ahead of the
patient, one behind. So Terry finally reached the mouth of the
Little Bighorn and found that the captain of the *Far West*
had managed to work the shallow-draft steamboat that far up
the Bighorn River. The wounded were carried aboard and
made as comfortable as possible, with a detail of their own
7th Cavalry men their nurses.

Then the moorings were loosened, the *Far West* swung
slowly around and down the Bighorn to the Yellowstone and
Fort Abraham Lincoln, bearing the news of the second wipe-
out of United States troops by the Sioux and their allies within
ten years.

8 RESUMÉ

★ ★ ★ ★ ★ ★ ★ ★

The Indian wars on the Plains differed from the usual military conflict, whether civil or between nations, in most aspects except one. As always, there were people who did not consider the warring inevitable. This time they could point to Canada, who took over her entire region without one battle with her Indians by the simple expedient of keeping her treaties. If more territory was to be appropriated from the natives, new treaties were negotiated, without subterfuge, force, or coercion. The United States broke most of her treaties before the ink on the Indian's X was dry.

The situation on the Plains was complicated by the wholesale destruction of the buffalo, the commissary of the Indians. Because the great herds, on Indian lands, were not only his sustenance and his religion but ethically, at least, his property, his anger was understandable. In the meantime the land-hungry pushed in for homes, the cattlemen for grass, the gold-seekers for treasure. Then in the early 1870's the depression dried up the financing of railroads headed into the west and Indian country through Kansas and the Dakotas. It was hoped that new gold strikes and railway access to old ones would lure reluctant investors. Besides, since the Civil War there was further intensification on the only remaining field of conflict— the rivalry for officerships in the shrinking army and the necessity to keep the Indians stirred up not only for war profits for the manufacturers and contractors but to advance the careers of the military.

From 1865 it had been clear that the Army of the Plains would be short-lived, with ambitious officers driven to jockeying for honors and victories to raise their rank and position, at least to hold their standing when the inevitable cuts came, and to further financial and business opportunities on retirement. To this end by 1867 the Plains had become a gaming field, a hunting ground for military trophies—victories over the Indians, particularly over bands with women and children, for warrior parties were difficult to locate and more difficult to strike, to defeat. Even with the avowed Extermination Policy of the government, there was usually some protest over the slaughter of helpless Indians and demands that the real culprits, the hostile warriors, be punished. Because peaceful villages were always easier to find, closer to the forts, trails, or agencies, unprepared for defense, and with fewer of the wilder, more daring young warriors, it was the peace Indians who were struck, with efforts to make them look like hostiles.

Out of this complicated Plains situation grew a sort of general disobedience of Plains officers, from colonels down the scale, usually with loud newspaper and magazine applause. Most of the men who hoped to further their ambitions in Indian warring, from Fetterman in 1866 through Reynolds the spring of 1876, were accused of disobeying orders. Royall, accused earlier, was charged with disobedience at the battle of the Rosebud only eight days before the Custer fight, and Merritt soon after the news of the Little Bighorn fight got out. He ignored General Crook's specific orders to hurry directly to him from the North Platte with supplies and reinforcements. Instead, he put off facing the hostile Sioux by swinging up around Red Cloud Reservation to intercept an older, more peaceful group finally driven out by starvation to take the treaty-guaranteed summer hunt. It happened to be a band of tame Cheyennes, mostly women and children and old men, a band peaceful enough to have remained this long around the hungry agency. Merritt's disobedience was aggrandized by King in his *Campaigning with Crook*, which the author had to withdraw for libel of a newspaper correspondent whom he called a coward, the reissued volume containing an abject apology, and admission by King that he had written from hearsay. He wasn't there at all.

With such Plains records, particularly Custer's own, including his suspension in 1867 and his arrest by Stanley on the Yellowstone in 1873, Terry could not have expected anything but the customary disobedience.

As for Custer's plan of battle, there is little to be said about that. The wide and worn trail should have warned so experienced a man that there were probably six to eight warriors for every trooper he had, warriors on fresh horses, fighting on their own terrain, for their homes and families. Further, Custer's scouts had tried to warn him of the great annual gathering up ahead and surely he had heard of the summer conferences at Bear Butte, so long a matter of common knowledge. The Medical History of Fort Laramie records that in 1834 Bull Bear brought one hundred lodges down from Bear Butte to trade at the new post on the North Platte River. In 1849, traders reported that the seven great council fires of the Teton Sioux were gathering there, and in 1857 word reached Washington that the great Teton council was meeting at Bear Butte to decide what must be done against the whites for Harney's attack on Little Thunder (now that the Indian year of mourning was over, as the Sioux told this author). In 1868 the commanding officer at Fort Laramie wrote of uneasiness about the big council of the Sioux, Northern Cheyennes, and Arapahos called to meet at Bear Butte. As usual even the Loaf About the Forts left Laramie to attend, anxious this year to discuss the government's request that the Loafers join the breeds on a reservation on the Missouri River, where all the Southern Tetons—the Brules and Oglalas—were eventually to go. The obligation of every band to be present at the great summer council while Custer pushed into the Black Hills in 1874 accounts for the lack of real resistance to his approach. The conference was always a time of counciling, from the smallest band to the chiefs of the seven divisions. Full attendance was encouraged, no war parties were permitted out.

So it was on the Little Bighorn, late June, 1876, now that there was no peace at Bear Butte any more. Everyone was to be there, no war parties were permitted against Crow or Shoshoni or Assiniboin, not even raiders against the gold-seekers heading to the Black Hills.

In the face of the evidence of the great trail before him, the advice of his scouts, Indian and white, and the knowledge he should have had of the ancient summer conference, Custer's division of his small force into three parts is inexplicable, unless one assumes that it was of overwhelming importance that neither Benteen nor Reno share in any victory. How the fight would have ended if the command had not been divided must remain pure speculation.* That the Indians were powerful

---

* Lt. Gen. P. H. Sheridan, C.O., Military Division of the Missouri, 1877, with account of Red Horse, Sioux in Custer fight, says if Custer had joined Reno and Benteen at the ford he "could have held his own, at least, and possibly defeated the Indians."

enough in numbers and in determination to defeat the entire force cannot be doubted; whether the worn horses of the troops were strong enough to carry any beyond the reach of the pursuing warriors is debatable. At best the carnage would have been appalling. The unit was, after all, planned for scouting, not for combat without reinforcements by infantry, more cavalry, and Gatling guns.

The charge that there was a great deal of whisky among the troops on the Little Bighorn, either in Reno's pocket or with the soldiers of Custer's battalion, seems untenable. It was probably limited largely to hip flasks and the medical stores. Girard seems to have had the most. According to rumors he, as a noncombatant civilian employee, carried whisky in his saddlebags instead of ammunition, whisky that he sold except, perhaps, the drink he gave to Charley Reynolds in the timber on the bottoms. The report that the Indians said Custer's men were drunk probably originated in the Sioux way of getting an abstract idea across, the result of misinterpretation by the literal-minded. Probably the Indians told the interviewers what was often said in the hearing of this author—that the troops acted drunk, meaning they acted excited and unreasoning. That there was whisky in the canteens seems unlikely too. This must have been another error of interpretation—the Indians probably meant the metal flasks that many of the troopers, particularly the officers, carried. It was customary for most men, even nondrinkers on the summer Plains, to have some whisky handy because it was considered a sort of specific for bowel cramps—either the so-called summer cholera or dysentery—as well as for snakebite. There were high possibilities of both in late June weather. Colonel Gibbon had an attack of something like dysentery on the Yellowstone. Rattlesnakes were common all over the Plains, and a particular menace to men fighting running foot battles, ducking into hollows, dropping behind bushes or banks with no time to look the ground over. The author found a rattlesnake skin on Calhoun Ridge as late as 1930.

As for Reno being drunk the night of the 25th—that story didn't get around until about 1879. Most army officers were drinkers of varying degree. The fact remains that Reno saved most of his force, no mean feat for a sober man, as the bodies strung out along the ridges and slopes far beyond him testify. One might argue that the passionate Custer partisans denigrated the regiment by their efforts to prove everyone but their hero guilty of the debacle on the Custer battleground. They even went to the extreme of gathering up a false affidavit from Mary Adams, colored maid of the Custers. In her statement she claimed to have overheard General Terry tell Custer at the mouth of the Rosebud, "Use your own judgment and do what you think best when you strike the trail, and whatever you do, Custer, hold onto your wounded."

It is highly unlikely that the illiterate Mary Adams would have remembered the exact words as late as January 16, 1878, the date of the affidavit. Besides, it has been proved that she was not at the mouth of the Rosebud at all in 1876, but had remained with Mrs. Custer at Fort Abraham Lincoln. There were dozens of other concocted stories, some inspired by Custer adherents, many of those seeking self-aggrandizement, including the seventy men who claimed to be survivors of the Custer fight that E. A. Brininstool, writer on Sioux and Custer topics, collected. The exaggerations, the violent partianship, did help push one section of the 7th Cavalry into the most barbaric conduct fourteen years later, when they mowed down women and children with Hotchkiss guns at Wounded Knee in 1890, shouting, some reported, "There's another blast for Custer!"

The 7th of the Plains was a great regiment and the common

trooper of it deserved a better reputation than he sometimes receives.

That large sums of money were taken by the Indians from the bodies of Custer's men is another fantasy. It is true that the colonel had prevented the paymaster from delivering the two months' pay at Fort Abraham Lincoln, apparently to keep Seip, the post trader, from getting it. Instead, the paymaster was ordered to accompany the expedition to the first camp, on Heart River, designated as Camp One. It was a sort of last farewell for some of the officers and their wives. Mrs. Custer and several others had come out with picnic hampers and camping equipment. The next day the mail was sent back by the returning escort, and no telling how many troopers sent money to families, friends, creditors, or to banks. At Camp Eight, two scouts were sent back with the mail. One of them, Red Bear, brought many letters and newspapers out a few days later, the first of several of these mail round trips.

It is known that a mail bag went in from the Powder River June 10 because it included a letter from Custer to his wife, with the usual outsider's remarks about the region. Certainly any man as long on the Plains as Custer knew better than to say they were in country that had never been visited by white men. It is clear that the Verendryes were there in 1742–43, and both Spaniards and Frenchmen long before them, with small trading posts at various nearby sites for a hundred years by 1876. Still, it is a revealing remark from the man who could never bear to be second.

By the time the column reached Camp Twenty on the Yellowstone, with the *Far West* anchored in the river, James Coleman had set up a large trader tent well stocked with the usual supplies requested by an army in the field. There was a large quantity of liquor, and apparently considerable sale.

Troopers drunken enough to warrant detention in a guardhouse were herded out upon the prairie and sobered up there. At frontier tent-saloon prices, the enlisted man's base pay of thirteen dollars a month would not cover much more than one good drunk.

Many bought so-called dry goods from Coleman—the large hats to keep the hot sun off and extra kerchiefs against the dust besides the little luxuries and necessities like salves, raisins, cigars and chewing tobacco, and candy.

To be sure, the gamblers of the 7th clung to some of their money for the games that had brought the 7th Cavalry some notice. These included several of the young officers who stayed up all the night of the 21st before the start along the Rosebud the next day.

There is substantial difference in the amount of distant firing reported by the men of Reno and Benteen, including Godfrey and Benteen, Varnum and Reno. One wonders if it was not more temporary war deafness on the part of one group and a refusal to understand the actual power of the Indian on the other—between the Reno men who had faced that power and were concerned with bare survival and those who came up after the bloody fight on the bottoms and the river and bluffs was about done, and understood nothing of the situation. Benteen, as an old campaigner, had some discernment, of course, and one could expect young Varnum, only four years out of West Point, to have ears as sharp as Godfrey's—except that Varnum's rang with the close gunfire that had scattered his scouts and wounded and killed his friends in the first hot encounter of his life, while Godfrey had been off on a quiet valley chase with Benteen. There was also the difference in sounds from as far off as four and a half miles, cut by river breaks, particularly with a cross-wind, no matter how light.

Besides, there was the urgency of the Indian attack, as well as differences in the interpretation of what was heard and exactly when. Those who argue against any validity in the Indian reports of the Custer battle because they vary a great deal should try to bring some agreement out of the white-man accounts. On even so elementary an aspect as the time of day, there is as much as four–five hours' difference.

So long as men of the time of Custer with the 7th Cavalry were alive, it was common out on the Plains to hear such conjecturing: Suppose Custer had managed a victory over a few Sioux June 1876, and got word of it to the Democratic Convention at St. Louis. How would Custer have run against Hayes for the presidency? Generally the verdict was that he would have made a better showing than Tilden. Custer was well aware that the nation gave the presidency to such men as Washington, Taylor, and Grant because they won her wars. Surely the man who ended the twenty years of Plains wars with the Indian would be no less rewarded. Besides, in 1876, aspiring to the presidency was still considered the privilege of every native male, not only the man with millions or high political position, but also the man with no money or political position as well. There was probably never a better year to stampede a political convention than at St. Louis in 1876, and who ever voted against a national hero?

There is a recurring interest in the presidency in Custer's juvenile letters and utterances from before West Point on, augmented powerfully by the colonel's success as a speaker from Johnson's presidential train, where he heard the cry not for Johnson but for Grant and Custer. Well, old Ulysses S. had his round, and now it was Custer's turn. He had listened to the suggestion several times in the fulsome praise of newspaper and railroad owners. Now the sense of destiny that often appears in youths intolerant of discipline and restraint was upon him, a sort of desperate destiny. The mood permeates all the speeches and flattery of the luncheons and dinners the winter of 1875–76 in New York. The later corroboration by the scouts in Libby's *The Arikara Narrative* came as no surprise to anyone who had followed the stories of the Indians and the white men of the Plains, or Custer's own writings. The *Narrative* is the story of the Ree scouts with Custer to the Little Bighorn, and contains their firsthand accounts of Custer's promises to Bloody Knife when he was made the Great Father, the President, if he could win even a little victory over a few Sioux.

Custer was very well aware that no one voted against a national hero.

APPENDIX

★ ★ ★ ★ ★ ★ ★ ★

(This list includes the names of enlisted men, as far as can be ascertained, with many of them illiterate and some hiding their identity.)

Benteen, Capt. Frederick W.
Bradley, Lt. James H.
Brisbin, Maj. James S.
Butler, Sergt. James
Calhoun, Lt. James
Cooke, Lt. Wm. W.
Crittenden, 2nd Lt. John J.
Crook, Brig. Gen. George
Culbertson, Sergt. Ferdinand A.
Curtis, Sergt. ———
Custer, Boston
Custer, Capt. Tom W.
Davern, Sergt. Edward
De Rudio, Lt. Chas. C.
De Wolf, Dr. ———
Edgerly, 2nd Lt. Winfield S.
Elliott, Maj. ———
Fetterman, Capt. Wm. J.
Finkle, Sergt. August
Finley, Sergt. Jeremiah

French, Capt. Thos. B.
Gibbon, Col. John
Gibson, Lt. Frank M.
Godfrey, Capt. Edward S.
Hare, 2nd Lt. Luther R.
Harney, Gen. Wm. S.
Harrington, 2nd Lt. Henry M.
Hazen, Col. Wm. B.
Hodgson, 2nd Lt. Benj. H.
Kanipe, Sergt. Daniel
Kellogg, Mark
Keogh, Capt. Miles W.
King, Lt. Charles
Lord, Dr. G. E.
Low, Lt. Wm. H., Jr.
Ludlow, Capt. Wm.
McDermott, Priv. ———
McDougall, Capt. Thos. M.
McIlhargy (or Ilhargey),
    Priv. Archibald

McIntosh, Lt. Donald
Martin, Trumpeter John
Mathey, Lt. Edward G.
Merrill, Maj. Lewis
Merritt, Col. Wesley
Mitchell, Priv. John
Moylan, Capt. Myles
O'Neal, (or O'Neil), Priv. Thos.
Porter, Dr. H. R.
Porter, Lt. James E.
Reed, Armstrong (Autie)
Reno, Maj. Marcus A.
Reynolds, Col. Joseph J.
Royall, Maj. Wm. B.

Ryan, Sergt. John M.
Sherman, Gen. Wm. T.
Smith, Lt. Algernon E.
Stanley, Gen. David S.
Sturgis, 2nd Lt. James G.
Sturgis, Col. S. D.
Tanner, Priv. James
Terry, Maj. Gen. Alfred H.
Varnum, Lt. Charles A.
Voight (or Vogt, Voit),
    Priv. H. C.
Wallace, Lt. Geo. D.
Weir, Capt. Thos. B.
Yates, Capt. Geo. W.

SELECTED BIBLIOGRAPHY
for the General Reader

Bourke, John G. *On the Border with Crook.* New York, Charles Scribner's Sons, 1891.

Brill, C. J. *Conquest of the Southern Plains.* Oklahoma City, Okla., Golden Saga Pubs., 1938.

Brininstool, E. A. *A Trooper with Custer.* Columbus, Ohio, Hunter-Trader-Trapper, 1926. Vol. I.

——. *Fighting Red Cloud's Warriors.* Columbus, Ohio, Hunter-Trader-Trapper, 1926. Vol. V.

Bureau of Ethnology, *Annual Reports.* Fourth and Tenth.

Byrne, P. E. *The Red Man's Last Stand.* London, 1927.

Clymer, Hiester. "Report on Management of the War Department, Rep. Hiester Clymer, Chairman of Committee," *House Reports* No. 799, 44th Cong. 1st Sess. Serial No. 1715 (1876), Vol. 8.

Custer, Elizabeth B. *Boots and Saddles.* New York, Harper and Brothers, 1885.

Custer, George A. *My Life on the Plains.* Chicago, Lakeside Press, 1952.

DeLand, Charles Edmund. *The Sioux Wars.* South Dakota Department of History Collections, Vols. XV and XVII. (Pierre, S.D.)

Dustin, Fred. *The Custer Tragedy.* Ann Arbor, Mich. Privately printed, 1939.

Finerty, John F. *War Path and Bivouac, or the Conquest of the Sioux.* Chicago, Donohue, Henneberry & Co., 1890.

Fougera, Katherine G. *With Custer's Cavalry*. Caldwell, Idaho, The Caxton Printers, Ltd., 1940.

Frost, Lawrence A. *The Custer Album: a Pictorial Biography of General George A. Custer*. Seattle, Wash., Superior Publishing Company, 1964.

Gibbon, Colonel John. "Last Summer's Expedition against the Sioux," *American Catholic Quarterly Review*, Vol. II (April, 1877).

———. "Hunting Sitting Bull," *American Catholic Quarterly Review*, Vol. II (October, 1877).

Graham, Colonel William A. *The Custer Myth: A Source Book of Custeriana*. Harrisburg, Pa., The Stackpole Co., 1953.

Grinnell, George B. *The Fighting Cheyennes*. New York, Charles Scribner's Sons., 1915.

Hawley, Paul R. "Did Cholera Defeat Custer?" *International Abstracts of Surgery*, Vol. 84 (May, 1947).

Hazen, W. B. *Some Corrections of Life on the Plains*. Norman, University of Oklahoma Press, 1962.

Keim, De Benneville R. *Sheridan's Troopers on the Frontier*. Philadelphia, David McKay, 1891.

King, Charles. *Campaigning with Crook*. New York, Harper and Brothers, 1890. [Reissued with apology for libelous material in earlier editions, 1891.]

Kuhlman, Charles. *Did Custer Disobey Orders at the Battle of the Little Big Horn?* Harrisburg, Pa., The Stackpole Co., 1957.

———. *Legend into History: The Custer Mystery*. Harrisburg, Pa., The Stackpole Co., 1951.

Libby, Orin G. (ed.). "The Arikara Narrative of the Campaign Against the Hostile Dakotas," *North Dakota Historical Collections*, Vol. VI (Bismarck, N.D., 1920).

Luce, Edward S., *Keogh, Comanche, and Custer*. St. Louis, Mo., J. S. Swift Co., Inc., 1939.

Maguire, Edward. "Explorations and Surveys in the Department of Dakota, 1876–'77," *Report of the Chief of Engineers for Fiscal Year ending June 30, 1877*. Appendix.

Marquis, Thomas B. *A Warrior Who Fought Custer*. Minneapolis, Midwest Book Co., 1931.
——. *She Watched Custer's Last Battle* [Katie Big Head]. Hardin, Mont. Privately printed, 1933.
Menninger, Karl. "A Psychiatrist Looks at Custer," *International Abstracts of Surgery*, Vol. 84 (May, 1947).
Merington, Marguerite. *The Custer Story*. New York, Devin-Adair Co., 1950.
Merril, Edward. *Auld Lang Syne*. Privately printed, n.d.
Mills, General Anson. *My Story*. Washington, D.C. Privately printed, 1918.
Neihardt, John G. *Black Elk Speaks*. New York, William Morrow & Company, 1932.
New York Herald, June 1 to August 31, 1876. [What one newspaper published.]
Parsons, John E., and DuMont, John S. *Firearms Used in the Custer Battle*. Harrisburg, Pa., The Stackpole Co., 1953.
Remsburg, John E., and George J. *Charley Reynolds*. Kansas City, Mo., H. M. Sender, 1931.
Reno, Marcus A. (defendant). *Reno Court of Inquiry: Abstract of the Official Record of Proceedings*. Preface by W. A. Graham. Harrisburg, Pa., The Stackpole Co., 1954.
Sandoz, Mari. *The Buffalo Hunters*. New York, Hastings House, 1954.
——. *Cheyenne Autumn*. New York, McGraw-Hill Book Co., Inc., 1953.
——. *Crazy Horse*. New York, Alfred A. Knopf, Inc., 1942.
Schmitt, Martin F. *General George Crook: His Autobiography*. Norman, University of Oklahoma Press, 1946.
Scott, Hugh L. *Some Memories of a Soldier*. New York, Century Company, 1928.
Sheridan, Phil H. *Records of Engagements with Hostile Indians, 1868–1882*. Washington, 1882.
Sturgis, Thomas. *Common Sense View of the Sioux War*. Waltham, Mass., Sentinel, 1877.
The Tepee Book (1916 and 1926, etc.)

United States War Department. *Annual Report, 1876:* Report of the General of the Army.

————. *Annual Reports, 1874, 1875, 1876, 1877:* Reports of the Secretary of War.

Van de Water, Frederick F. *Glory Hunter: A Life of General Custer.* Indianapolis, Ind., The Bobbs-Merrill Company, 1934.

Vestal, Stanley. *Sitting Bull: Champion of the Sioux.* Boston, Houghton Mifflin Co., 1932.

————. *Warpath: True Story of the Fighting Sioux.* Boston, Houghton Mifflin Co., 1934.

Wheeler, Homer W. *Buffalo Days.* Indianapolis, Ind., The Bobbs-Merrill Company, 1925.

Whittaker, Frederick. *A Complete Life of Gen. George A. Custer.* New York, Sheldon, 1876.

INDEX

★ ★ ★ ★ ★ ★ ★ ★

New York *Herald*, 19, 131, 162
No Flesh, 128

Old She Bear, 65 and note
O'Neal, Pvt. Thomas, 158

Porter, Dr. H. R., 86, 99, 149, 154, 158
Porter, Lt. James E., 43, 106

Red Bear, 179
Red Horn Bull, 80
Red Horse, 80
Red Star, 52, 53
Reed, Armstrong, 14, 50, 107
    death of, 127
Reno, Major Marcus A., 16, 29, 43, 158, 178
    given a command, 63
    ordered to attack, 66–67
    past history of, 68
    reaches Little Bighorn, 69–70
    sends message to Custer, 71–72
    charges Sioux, 72–75
    sends second message to Custer, 73
    battle begins, 75–78
    retreats across river, 79–86
    digs in, 87–88
    joined by Benteen, 94–95
    tries to obtain water, 99–101
    driven back to Reno Hill, 132–135
    besieged by Indians, 136–149
    leads countercharge, 150–151
    holds out, 152–155
    moves to new position, 157–158
    meets Gen. Terry, 159–160
Reynolds, Charles, 14, 41, 45, 52, 55, 69, 80, 82
Ryan, Sgt. John M., 86, 143

Seventh Cavalry Regiment, 13, 47, 81, 83, 125, 161, 178

Sheridan, Lt. Gen. P. H., 176 n.
Sherman, Gen. William T., 15, 19, 27
Sioux Indians, 15, 24, 39, 48, 58, 80, 136
    religious practices of, 38, 127
    prepare for attack, 113–114
    attack Custer, 119–125
    victory, 126–128
    attack Benteen, 132–155
    leave the scene, 156
Sitting Bull, 23, 38, 58
Smith, Lt. Algernon E., 106, 126
Stabbed (medicine man), 42, 53
    magic rites, 59–60
Strikes Two, 65
Sturgis, 2nd Lt. James G., 106, 122
    death of, 171
Sturgis, Col. S. D., 26

Tanner, Pvt. James, 151
Taylor, Muggins, 160
Terry, Brig. Gen. Alfred H., 13, 16, 25, 29, 160, 172
Tilden, Samuel J., 130

Varnum, Lt. Charles A., 14, 45, 70, 71, 86, 95, 180
    at Crow's Nest, 50–53
Voight, Pvt. H. C., 151

Wallace, Lt. George D., 22, 67, 78
Weir, Capt. Thomas B., 18, 63, 89
    argues with Reno, 98–99
White Cloud, 38
White Swan, 107

Yates, Frank, 106
Yates, Capt. George W., 18, 58, 106–107, 126
Young Black Moon, 80
Young Hawk, 65, 136, 141